THE CRY

THAT

WASN'T HEARD

By

E. Nadine Thaxton-Tensley

Copyright © 2005 E. Nadine Thaxton-Tensley
All rights reserved. No part of this publication may be reproduced, stored in a retrieval system, or transmitted in any form or by any means, electronic, mechanical, photocopying, recording, or otherwise, without the prior written permission of the publisher.

ISBN: 0-9772296-8-8

Published by:
Holy Fire Publishing
531 Constitution Blvd. Martinsburg, WV 25401
www.ChristianPublish.com

Cover Design: Jay Cookingham

Printed in the United States of America and the United Kingdom

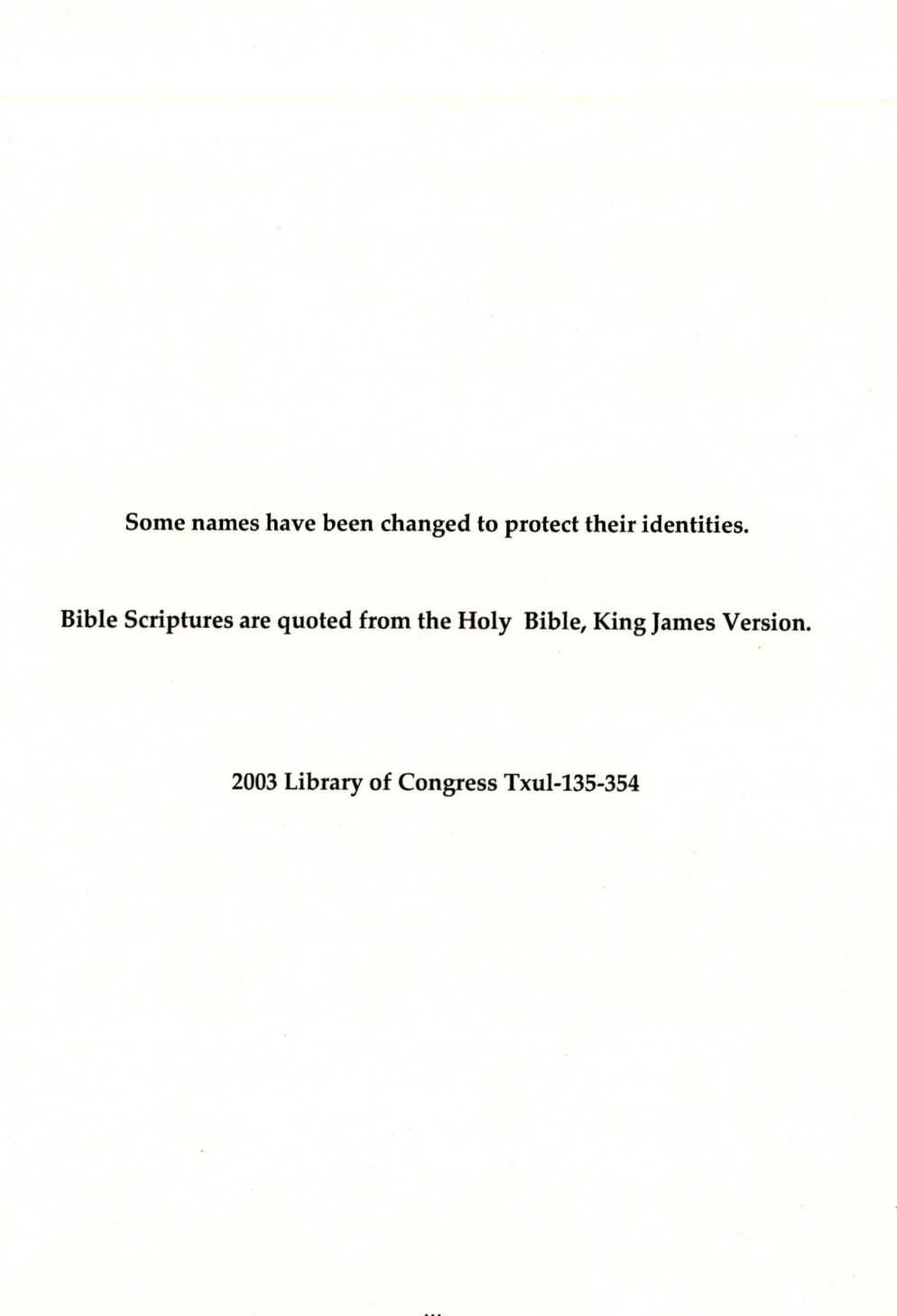

Some names have been changed to protect their identities.

Bible Scriptures are quoted from the Holy Bible, King James Version.

2003 Library of Congress Txul-135-354

A SPECIAL NOTE OF LOVE

TO MY HUSBAND LEWIS WHO GAVE HIS LIFE IN VIETNAM

ON JULY 29, 1970 IN AN EXPLOSION. HONEY YOU WERE AND ALWAYS WILL BE A TRUE SOLDIER.

MANY YEARS HAVE COME AND GONE BUT NEVER A DAY WITHOUT WARM THOUGHTS OF YOU.

DEDICATIONS

FATHER, SON, & HOLY SPIRIT: Who is first in my life. Thanks for creating in me a new heart and abiding in me. I will always give **YOU** the praise. **My Loving Daughter:** Life hasn't been easy for us but having you for a daughter has made it worth while. **My Devoted Sister:** I now know from whence the meaning of sister came, thanks for being mine. **My Precious Niece, Nephew and Great Nephew:** Thanks for your love and sense of humor. Keep on smiling; you are that special ray of sunshine in my life. **My Caring Aunt and late Uncle:** You were that "ram in the bush," I'm most grateful. **My Miracle Friend:** It was God and you who reshaped my life. I will forever be indebted to you for your alliance. Many thanks. To all of my family, friends and foes that made my life a story worth sharing I affably thank you. God Bless you all.

AN HONORABLE ACKNOWLEDGMENT

A special homage to all of the brave men and women of the United States Armed Forces who have and still is serving our country so assiduously.

To the many families who have suffered great losses and heartaches. I am walking in your shoes. This is a wound that time has not been able to heal. Be assured that we are not suffering in vain.

To all the children who were not given the opportunity to know their parents, I pray that you will seek forgiveness in your hearts for our leaders and our adversaries and find reconciliation in knowing that your parents fought for a safe country in which you are free to live and learn.

Let us all remember that this is a perfect world. It is the actions of the hearts and hands of our fellow man who causes the needless bloodshed.

MAY GOD BLESS US ALL

PSALM 27

A PSALM OF DAVID

The Lord is my light and my salvation; whom shall I fear? The Lord is the strength of my life; of whom shall I be afraid?

When the wicked, even mine enemies and my foes, came upon me to eat up my flesh, they stumbled and fell.

Though a host should encamp against me, my heart shall not fear, though war should rise against me, in this will I be confident.

One thing have I desired of the Lord, that will I seek after, that I may dwell in the house of the Lord all the days of my life, to behold the beauty of the Lord, and to enquire in his temple.

For in the time of trouble he shall hide me in his pavilion; in the secret of his Tabernacle shall he hide me: he shall set me upon a rock.

And now shall mine head be lifted up above mine enemies round about me: therefore will I offer in his tabernacle sacrifices of joy; I will sing, yea, I will sing praises unto the Lord.

Hear, O Lord, when I cry with my voice: have mercy also upon me, and answer me.

When thou saidst, Seek ye my face; my heart said unto thee, Thy face, Lord, will I seek.

Introduction

THE CRY THAT WASN'T HEARD

"The Cry That Wasn't Heard" is a pious, therapeutic, must share, semi-autobiography of a young black girl who was born on a farm in rural North Carolina. Her young life was continuously being attacked through deaths and adversities. Following the death of her mother she and her elder sister were unofficially adopted by elderly distant cousins, where a solid spiritual foundation was laid. The miles covering her life's highway were not only long but they were filled with disappointments and abuse. Her trails forced her to mature faster than her years.

It wasn't until her move to Washington, DC that some stability was fashioned. Even so, she became a wife, mother and widow before the age of twenty. Straying and nearly crumbling under the many pressures, she received guidance through visions and dreams of her deceased love ones. It was God through celestial encounters along with God's spirit through a friend who enabled her to return to her humble beginnings. Her world was restored miraculously.

Her love and concern for others inspired her to become a missionary and later an evangelist, often opening her heart and home to those who were in need of a helping hand.

"The Cry" was written as a three-fold ministry. First as therapy for the writer. Remembering the past and seeing it in writing helps to sort the good from the bad and accepting it all as a doorway through life. Second, for direction seekers. Our paths have been preordained. Learn to trust the inner (spiritual) man. Have faith in knowing that "greater is He that is in you, than he that is in the world." 1 John 4:4 Third, for the young, broken hearted, seemingly hopeless generation, mainly the minorities and the underdogs. There is "NO" situation that's beyond repair. Stay in the race and fight a virtuous fight. We were never promised an easy struggle but we are promised victory through Christ Jesus.

Conquering trials may be arduous but they will be appreciated in the end. One will never know the outcome of a circumstance until the task has been completed. "The Cry" was not just a task, but a victorious one.

Table of Contents

A Special Note of Love

Dedications

Acknowledgments

Scripture of Strength

Introduction

PART ONE: THE STRUGGLES OF A SOUL

Good Night Mama

The Spirit Moved

Hell Was Loved Out Of Me

I Can't Fight Anymore

Big City Bright Lights

My Soldier's Prayer

PART TWO: VICTORY IS MINE

Raised From The Dead

My Missing Rose

Good-bye Daddy

My Eyes Have Seen The Glory

Author Biography

PART ONE: THE STRUGGLES OF A SOUL

CHAPTER ONE

When my way grows drear, precious Lord, linger near,
When my life is almost gone; hear my cry, hear my call,
Hold my hand lest I fall; Take my hand, precious Lord
Lead me home.

THOMAS A. DORSEY

More than a half-century has passed and my thoughts and memories are as vivid today as when I was just a little more than a toddler playing on the front porch with my elder sister, Little Bit. We were catching raindrops from the old tin roof as we swung on the dilapidated, rickety swing hanging from the rafters of the porch by a rusty chain that could have snapped any moment. Frightened by the height I would jump from the swing as it lowered, only to hop on again following Little Bit's many promises not to swing so high. As we played, a steady flow of people, both blacks and whites from various churches and nearby neighborhoods, kept coming and going. Many were bringing flowers or food but almost everyone had their Bibles.

I particularly recall one tall heavy-set, silver haired woman sporting her Bible under one arm as she strutted toward the swing. She cooed. "Ooh my, what pru'ty lit'le guls you is."
Little Bit and I started laughing and poking fun. Least bothered by our laughter she continued talking as she leaned over to hug and kiss us. Little Bit, unlike me was always the courteous and shy one. She stood, bowed and hugged the woman; nearly smothering herself in the huge "V" shaped mounds as she thanked the woman for her altruistic compliment. It was quite evident that Little Bit was just thankful to be released. When the woman stretched her arms toward me, I stood, placed my hands on my hips, protruded my chest, slowly whirled in front of her and answered her coo. "Ooh my!, I is pre'ty ain't I?"
"Well!, if you ain't a sassy lit'le cuss," was her riposte. Quickly she turned and went inside.

Suddenly the storm worsened. The clouds turned dark. The thunder boomed loudly and the rain came down in a torrent. Everyone was scrambling for cover as they ran from their cars. Lightening was the only source of light. The yard became a lagoon in a matter of minutes.

Daddy had been waiting and watching for Rev. Earl, the family minister. Just as he stepped through the front door onto the

porch the short, pot-bellied distinguished looking minister stepped on the porch. Shedding his rain gear on a nearby chair, the minister greeted Daddy with a handshake. In dismay Daddy muttered. "Rev., things ain't no better, we done reached our end." The minister tried to offer words of hope but Daddy continued. "No. The doctor done been here already. He told me so. He even said that it ain't no need in calling him again."
As they reached the swing the minister gave us a gentle pat on our heads. Daddy took me in his arms and Little Bit by the hand. Teary eyed and a cracking voice he whispered, "Come on babies, let's go inside. Your mama wants to see you."

    The terrible storm had interrupted our electricity. Mama's bedroom was the front room just left of the hallway. Entering her room was frightening. Shadows of faces from the flickering flames of the kerosene lamps that sat on her bedside tables were indeed an unfriendly sight. An old Spiritual Hymn was being softly sung and hummed by the women sitting around the room. As we approached Mama's bed, she looked up at us but was too weak to lift her arms. With very short breaths and a whispery voice she managed to utter, "My--ba--bies, my pre--cious lit--le an-gels. Yo'--mama's--so--ti'ed. I must--go-rest--now. You--be--goo-d girls. Al--ways--'mem---ber --that God--loves you and I love--you to. Good--bye---for now-babies. We--will--meet--a-gain some-day--if you--

live-right."

Her head rolled to one side away from us. Rev. Earl placed his right hand on her forehead and began to pray; releasing her soul back to the Lord. The women continued humming softly and waving their hands; as unto the Lord. Daddy started fumbling in his pocket for his handkerchief as the same heavyset woman took me from his arms and carried us to the kitchen for a snack. By lantern light we had milk and cookies as she explained that Mama had gone to live with the Lord.

I wasn't sure of what she was telling us but I knew all along that something was wrong. Mama had been bed-ridden for sometime. It was for this reason that we had been brought here days earlier. Mama could barely walk when Daddy loaded us in his pick-up, threw a few of our belongings in the back of the truck and headed up the highway. Only when I asked if we were leaving home did he offer an explanation.

"No. I'm just taking yo'll up cut'n Charlie's and cut'n Martha's to stay awhile. I've got to be satisfied that yo'll chil'rens and your mama is cared for while I work." Mama's illness must have taken a turn for the worst. The previous days I'd noticed that Daddy had not gone to work. He never left Mama's bedside.

The following days seemed an eternity and extremely tormenting for Daddy. He tried to suppress his uncertain emotions, yet, there were times when he just couldn't. Ma Martha in all her wisdom always knew the right words to say that helped him through his melancholy days.

There was hardly a private moment. Both yards had become open reception areas. Visitors continued to come and go, well into the night. Many were still bringing food and soft drinks as they sat around eating and reminiscing of years past.

Little Bit and I entertained the children that came with their parents. This was a pleasure for us because the only times we got together with other children were when our cousins came around or at church and there we knew to behave like trained soldiers.

On the night of the wake Mama's body was viewed all night. The silver, white-satin lined casket sat in the front hallway surrounded by an array of colorful floral arrangements as viewers strolled by. Comments were being made on how well and peaceful she looked. "She doesn't look like she has had a sick day in her life." That's what nearly everyone was saying. Dressed in a sky blue chiffon shroud, clinching a single white rose, she gripped a slight smile that brightened her face as though she lay sleeping. "Your mama is gone to sleep and will be sleeping forever."
Was what Daddy told us as he lifted us so we could tell her good night.

We were taken upstairs and tucked in for the night. Before

going to bed we always had to say our prayers. This night wasn't my usual prayer. I asked a favor from God. "Please God, wake my mama so we can be together again and go back to our own home." This plea wasn't meant to be.

Morning came much too soon. I felt as though I had just fallen to sleep when Little Bit and I were awakened by the sounds of people still engaging in visitation. The women were working in the kitchen, brewing coffee, banging pots and pans as they served breakfast. We wondered if anyone else had gone to bed at all.

It wasn't long before Daddy entered our room. One look at his face confirmed that he had not gotten any sleep. His eyes were swollen and red. He placed a tub with water in the middle of the floor. Behind him was a charming young lady with a tray of food. Daddy hugged us and gave us the agenda for the day. He then pointed toward a dress bag hanging on the door as he asked the lady if she would bathe and dress us for him. Her expression showed that she was eager and willing to assist Daddy. In an alluring move she assured him that she would take good care of us. She introduced herself to us and partook in some chitchat as she served us breakfast. After which, Little Bit took her bath while I was getting my hair combed. She was the perfect stepmother candidate, hopeful.

We were dressed alike; all white dresses, socks, ribbons,

patent leather shoes and purses with lace gloves stuffed in our purses.

When we went downstairs a multitude of people greeted us. They had gathered to share in the final prayer before leaving for the church. Murmuring could be heard throughout the house as people were asking questions concerning Little Bit's and my welfare. A few single ladies were talking among themselves as well. They had "welfare concerns" of their own. One "male seeker" plainly declared. "He will never have a lonely moment if I can help it." The one who dressed us threw in her lustful comment before they conveniently made their way to Daddy offering their surefire sympathy with a hint of desire. Their intensions weren't comprehensible to me but I sensed that they were trying to get close to Daddy and I would never allow them to use such a gathering to propose ways to steal from me. Although, Daddy was a tall good-looking man who possessed whatever it was that drove women into tail spins whenever he entered the room, now he was too grief-stricken to welcome their advances.

There was another group, the old, nosey, signifying ones. From their appearances they should have been busy making reservations in the cemetery for themselves.
"Wh're's de chil'en gonna stay?" Asked an elderly woman a few feet ahead of us. An even older man scratching his head as if he

was going to make the final decision replied.

"Well, I hones'ly don't know, but I'll say dis shere, da Sanders's too ol' to tak' in chil'ens dis siz' and his mammy and pappy is to."

Another woman added her unsolicited damning judgment. "Who-so-eva tak'em in will sho' nough hav' a han' ful. Specia'ly dat youn'est one; 'cause she's a pistol now, and ain't fou' yet."

I knew that she was talking about me and I tried to think of a way to get even with her but before I could retaliate Rev. Earl came forward and approached Daddy with his sincere concerns.

"Son, I know that you are going through a lot right now but have you given any thought as to who will be helping with the girls?"

Daddy paused. Seeking the minister's approval, he cautiously answered. "Well, yes sir. I'll be leaving them here with Cut'n Charlie and Cut'n Martha. They asked for them the other day after Anna died."

The minister displayed his endorsement with a saintly smile and replied. "Son, you have made a wise decision. Your wife must be rejoicing in heaven right now, because it was right here, in this very house that she was raised when her mother passed. Bro. Deacon and Sis. Saunders did a wonderful job with her and so will they do with your girls."

To stop all the speculations and to shut the busy mouths the minister got everyone's attention. Before making the announcement he gave a brief sermon on love.

"You all should know that love is not measured by one's age, but by one's deeds. I've heard your negative murmuring. More important, so has God. He is not pleased with your comments or assumptions. I must warn you that it is your Christian duty to uphold, love and pray for this family."

Guilt and condemnation were so prevalent it could be felt and seen, even by me. The minister continued with his rapturous announcement.

"These motherless children will be staying right here with Deacon and Sister Saunders. This is where they belong. I know that this home have a solid spiritual foundation that's constructed of pure love."

Rev. Earl turned and hugged Daddy, then knelt and hugged us collectively, before initiating the final prayer.

Following the benediction everyone fell in line behind the ministers. Daddy first, escorted by a nurse was led to the family car. Little Bit and I walked behind them with a nurse and were taken to the same car. The Saunders accompanied us. Everyone else followed and got in their private cars.

Once in the family car I climbed on Daddy's knees. Looking through the back window, the procession seemed endless as it slowly moved up the highway in route to the church. I looked toward the sky. I saw an image of Mama in the clouds. Her face was glowing as though the sun was shining through it. Her spirit was in a rolling motion but that didn't stop Mama from following "her little girls", nor did it destroy her silhouette. She was blowing kisses through the clouds. A part of me wanted to share Mama's visit with Daddy and Little Bit but I didn't. I took this as "my" private last moments. It was this moment that I realized this is final. God did not hear my cry. He is not going to wake Mama. We are not going to be together anymore. She has already gone to rest and her remains will go in the cold ground; never to be seen again.

Arriving at the church and seeing cars already parked, I immediately became angry and felt a sense of betrayal. I was thinking that everyone should have come to the house and left with us. I wanted the three of us to be the first to go in "this service." After all, this was a service for "my mama". I sadly turned and looked forward.

The big black hearse had stopped at the steep church steps and the family car in which we were riding had parked behind it. Before we were ushered out we watched the coffin and flowers being carried up the steps into the church.

Stepping from the limo and hearing the heavenly voices of the choir singing Mama's favorite songs of Zion quickly subdued my anger.

CHAPTER TWO

I. E. received his name from Little Bit. She could not pronounce Char-lie. A short, medium built, bald, jovial "fellow" who walked with a slight limp. He loved to read the Bible and tell biblical stories, adding his own heartfelt versions to bring them to a child's understanding. The most inspiring story was his version of God's Creation.

One serene afternoon we were all relaxing. Little Bit and I were on the floor playing a board game. Ma Martha was sitting in her rocker working on a quilt and I. E. was sitting in the corner reading his Bible. All of a sudden, looking over his wire rimmed glasses and full of excitement he cleared his throat and spoke out. "You know one thing girls? God is good!" He'd clearly gotten our attention. We dropped our game pieces, sat up and turned toward him.

"Let me tell you'll just how good He really is! He thought of us 'wa-a-ay' back, even before there was a world! You see, it all started with God sitting on His throne. He was awful lonely sitting up there looking out into space and seeing nothing but darkness."

Rubbing his chin as if he was indeed thinking on something important he continued.

"One day God called a meeting among Himself. At that meeting He confessed. 'How selfish of Me to keep all this space for Myself.'"

Leaning backward in his straight leg chair he started stretching his arms in the many directions to demonstrate God's conversation.

'With all this space, I can divide it into two parts. The top part could be the sky so bright and pleasing to the sight. My smile will shine through giving warmth and light. In the stillness of the night, I'll glow and sparkle through the moon and the stars. The bottom half could be the earth, enough ground for My people to live and play There could be trees, big and small, rivers, deep and wide. Yes, this could be a beautiful world for my people.' Taking a second look into space, He looked thousands of years into the future, there He spotted two little girls standing afar off. 'Ummmm,' He said to Himself. 'I believe that is Little Bit and Dee Dee that I see standing over yonder.' Straining His eyes to see through all that darkness, He said, 'yes, it is them. They are due to be born many years from now. I'd better get to work and make this a beautiful world for them. Indeed, a beautiful world for two beautiful girls. They will grow up and thank Me someday. Meeting adjourn.'

I.E. slapped the side of his chair with his hand as God's gavel.

After listening to his story I crawled to my knees, leaned on his lap and asked, "I.E., did God really build this world just for us?" Placing his arms around the both of us he answered. "Yes He did, my child. Yes He did. He did this for all of us and we mustn't EVER forget it!"

Ma Martha obtained her name from me. I tried to call her Mama Martha but the second "ma" was never sounded. She was a beautiful, slender, average height, very astute woman with long salt and pepper hair that was worn in either a ball drawn to the back or two side braids crossed in the back. More than ten years I.E.'s junior, she was very affectionate and caring. They never had children of their own but were impregnated with a natural gift and love for raising them.

We immediately became one happy family. They were both very religious. Without a doubt God was first in their lives. They were always singing and praying. They would get "happy" anywhere, wherever the spirit moved them.

Our large white stucco, two story house sat along the highway with a front porch the length of the house. One end of the porch was decorated with our swing and the other was adorned with Ma Martha's potted plants which she talked to daily as lovingly as she did with us. They returned her love with real beauty and sweet fragrances. Gorgeous multi-colored rose bushes bejeweled both corners of the house. Summer shade was the huge aging oak trees surrounded by well manicured hedges in the front yard. The back yard was as expansive, encompassing a shed connecting the corn crib. In inclement weather I.E. kept his antique hand cranked Ford under the shed along with his tractor.

Just beyond the hog pen was the stable that housed the horses and cows. A large pasture was fenced off with barbed wire. The tobacco barn stood below the house, also along the highway.

As far as could be seen were fields of crops. Vegetables, tobacco, corn and wheat were the major corps. Along the south side was an orchard, fruits of all kinds and colors. Anyone traveling along the highway was welcomed to the self-service "market place." Some would ask first; others, especially the ones who knew us would help themselves then stop by the house for a visit, offering a dollar or two. Ma Martha never accepted any money. "Help yourself," she'd gladly say. "Because we have no use for them all anyhow." She was right about that. After all the sharing, marketing, canning, drying and preserving we still had bushels of fruits and vegetables to feed the hogs, many more would fall to the ground and rot.

Pork salad and watercress grew in the wild. Pork salad mostly grew in moist rich soil; around the hog pen. This was mainly used for medicinal purposes. At least once per year Ma Martha would serve a "mess" of Pork salad to clean our bodies of any impurities. Neighbors helped themselves to that as well, cutting it down by the stalk. Watercress grew out in the fields. Ma Martha would gather it by the baskets full, as though she had planted it herself.

We also raised strawberries and watermelons. From a child's viewpoint, one could never appreciate fresh fruit until you have sat in a cherry or peach tree; in a watermelon or strawberry patch and eat 'til your heart's content in the coolness of the dawning hours while they are still wet with dew. This much gratification was well worth all the spankings and I received many.

Black owned farms were scarce. Most blacks were either renters or sharecroppers, having no say in the business matters. I.E. and Ma Martha had actually purchased their farm but ironically it was adjoining Ma Martha's family farm. She and her brother Robert, who lived in the next house with his wife Mabel, purchased their siblings' shares and formed a partnership. I dare not say that they were rich but they certainly didn't want for anything. Ma Martha held the purse strings in our household and stingy she was. She had to have been the world's most frugal person. Not trusting banks she guarded her own private vault. Standing in the hallway was an old wardrobe with a top that could be lifted for entry. Her designer flour sacks separated her money according to denominations. The larger bills were placed at the bottom. She embroidered each bag with bright colored threads as her unique way of identifying the denominations.

Whatever her logic was, she rarely exchanged coins for bills. As the bags dry rotted the coins turned green with mold. She'd scrub the coins with Ajax, only then would she make new bags, reducing some weight by spending coins in the grocery store. Inside the wardrobe was where she kept her Sunday suits and "ready cash." A certain amount of paper money was rolled together and stuffed in an old sock then placed in a suit pocket. Not much was spent on food because mostly everything was raised on the farm.

A typical weekday started with Ma Martha rising hours before daybreak. The aromas of coffee brewing, bread baking, ham or herring frying, beans or greens boiling would wake everyone else. She would have three meals cooking at once. When her cooking was done she milked the cows and fed the hogs by lantern light before serving and joining us for breakfast. By daylight she would be ready to go out in the fields.

I. E., also using a lantern, moved slowly through his routine as he whistled his praises. He would replenish the woodbin from the woodpile out back, draw fresh water from the well in the back yard and feed the horses. Due to his age he didn't do any field work. Most of his days were spent sitting in the doorway of the corn crib shelling corn for the chickens as he talked and sang to the

Lord. An old "rat gnawed" Bible was kept in the crib and every once in a while he'd pull it out and read a scripture.

The Saunders were highly respected by all. Blacks and whites referred to them as Mr. Charlie or Mr. Saunders, Mrs. Martha, or Mrs. Saunders. Never can I recall hearing anyone address them by their first names. Neither was formally educated but they were considerably intelligent. The Bible and the newspapers which were delivered to our driveway daily was a reading tutor for them. They both knew how to research words in their well used dictionary. Every night I. E. read the newspapers, sharing the news with Ma Martha before reading the Bible and praying.

Farm help was plentiful and was offered by both races. During planting and harvesting seasons the farm was mostly maintained by "hired help," however, the term "hired help" never arose. The Saunders's unassuming nature enabled them to consider the help as people being generous. On any given day as they were paying the helpers they thanked them for their "great generosity."

I.E.'s greeting "comebacks" are hardly forgettable. When asked how he was doing his two most favorite replies were, "oh, I'm fair to middling," or "tolerable fair". He never failed to add "with the help of the Good Lord."

Uncle Robert's job took him to Petersburg, Virginia where he worked building highways. He'd come home some week-ends. One day while on his job he was in a near fatal accident. Blasting with dynamite he was accidentally blown up and was hospitalized for more than a year. Following his discharge he retired on disability, limiting his farm work.

Aunt Mabel was an over weight, mouthy, know-it-all. She did days work in Danville, Virginia, helping on the farm on her days off. Ma Martha and Aunt Mabel didn't exactly "set horses" but Ma Martha was never a complainer. She would come in from the field thanking God for the day's end as she prayed for a better tomorrow.

Farm life became fascinating for Little Bit and me. Sometime before we awoke Ma Martha would place two wash pans of water in our room and lay out our outfits for the day. After washing up and dressing we would rush down stairs, ready to eat and start our "busy" day, only to be stopped by I. E. "Girls, never start a day until you pray." He would read what seemed to be the longest scripture in the book; prayed an even longer prayer. He prayed for the world, everyone and everything in it. If by chance the "spirit moved" and they "got happy" we had to wait until they "praised the Lord", then everyone had to recite a Bible verse before we could eat. Little Bit and I laughed and did our "praising" to. Not understanding the Holy Spirit, we thought they were and having "fits." As much as we hated to endure the "happy acts" we looked forward to mealtimes. All meals were full of hugs, conversations and most of all love. Regardless of the amount of work there was to be done, family time was never spared. They praised us when we ate all of our food. They really got enjoyment out of watching us being happy.

We were taught the importance of earning a living and having your own at an early age. One of our jobs was to keep the water cold for the field workers. Sitting at the edge of the field was a stone keg with one dipper and everyone drank from it. Throughout the day Little Bit and I kept ice and water in the jug; using our molasses pails. Our salary depended on the number of trips that we made. The more trips that we made, the less money per trip. I'm sure that they had an amount already in mind for our days work. The pennies and nickels mounted.

Knock off time for lunch was high noon. Everyone came to our house and sat around under the big walnut tree in the back yard. Ma Martha served each one, the first plate always went to I.E. Before anyone took a morsel they knew to wait for I. E.'s prayer. An hour rest period came after lunch. Some took a nap there on the ground. Unless the work was finished early, the work day ended when the sun went down, near nighttime.

Our real money maker was peddling. One a week; usually Wednesdays, we would have family day in town. The evening before was spent gathering vegetables and fruits to carry to town. Ma Martha would pull out her old churn; allowing us turns agitating the milk with a long wooden stick with a cross at one end. When the butter formed on top of the milk she would collect it and mold it in half or whole pounds; placing them in the freezer until morning. Having everything gathered, washed, packed and sitting on the porch to keep cool, Ma Martha called drill time. She had us repeating every item for sell over and over again until it became a song.

Before going to bed we got our baths and hair combed. Sometimes we had corn rows, but if Ma Martha decided to wrap our hair we had to dye white tobacco strings with black shoe polish. To keep it in tack she pulled a silk stocking over her skilled work. Our prayers were said and hugs were shared before the lights went out. Little Bit and I couldn't readily fall asleep. We would lay there discussing how we wanted to spend our money the following day.

Ma Martha got up as usual, did her chores, then loaded the car. Leaving very little space for us. On these days our breakfast was light, usually milk and toast. However, she made sure that our growing appetites wouldn't suffer. We each had a shoebox with our name on it for a lunch box. She had taken much pride in preparing our snacks. We had fried chicken, homemade biscuits, a piece of fruit and a dessert of some kind. When all the preparations were finished and we were dressed in our pastel dresses with straw hats that tied under the chin with matching ribbons, I. E. would come in the room and lean back, pulling on his suspenders, he'd boast about his three favorite girls. He always hugged us and told us how pretty we looked.

After several turns of the crank handle, the car started. I. E. drove as slow as he walked. If that wasn't annoying enough they prayed and sang all the way to town. I imagine the trip took approximately an hour and a half. Little Bit and I would fall asleep, wake up and eat. If Little Bit fell asleep first I would eat her food too.

Our arrival in town was just as the townspeople were starting their day. I was eager to start peddling. We had a certain street from which we always started, working our way to our regular customers. Many had placed their orders the week before. Jumping from the car I'd run to a door and ring the bell. Little Bit, too shy to speak loud or distinctly, often stood back and watched. Usually it was the maid who answered the door. Immediately I started my song.

"Good morning ma'am.

Would you like to buy any tomatoes, potatoes, black-eyed peas, string beans, greens, onions, corn, berries, cherries, apples, peaches, watermelons, cantaloupes, butter or eggs?"

After checking with the lady of the house, she would return and place an order. It was rare for a household not to purchase something. Many would tip liberally, even invite us in for a cold drink or snack. Whether it was the maid or the lady of the house inviting us in, we were always asked to "come to the back door." I was introduced to Dr. Pepper and cream cheese on a bagel on our peddling trips.

    Finances were not our only gain from peddling; we actually made a few friends. Our birthdays and Christmases were always remembered. Gifts, some quite costly; like the set of children's encyclopedias, other learning aides, radios, clothes and household goods were given to us.

    There were a few bad experiences. The one that stayed in my craw for a long time was the encounter with a malicious white woman. I rang her doorbell in hopes of making a sell. She chased us from her door, calling us "black monkeys." We were frightened to tears as we ran back to the car. Always forgiving, Ma Martha kissed our tears away and assured us of our safety.

"It's alright babies, she's without any learning. She just showed her up-bringing. The Good Lord will handle her in due time." That was Ma Martha's rectifying way.

Like our farm work, Little Bit's and my salary depended upon what we were given from each item sold. I don't believe that we ever received less than five cent for any sale. We were allowed to keep all tips; at least for a little while. More often than not, they were more than our salaries.

Family day in town wouldn't be complete without making our two regular stops. Our first stop was the ice cream factory. The glass structure gave us the opportunity to watch the ice cream being made. There was a sitting area inside but we never experienced that luxury. Our seat was on the ground, under a shade tree along the sidewalk. I.E. sat in the car with his feet on the ground while Ma Martha went to get the ice cream through a service window which was cut in a front glass panel, before joining us on the ground. Enjoying the breeze, sights and good old fashion ice cream validated our own little world. This was also the spot where we counted our monies. Of course, I always earned the most. We poured our coins on the ground; including all tips. First, we had to take out our church money for Sunday. Then we separated our savings from "fun" money. With the exception of a dollar or two, we had to turn everything over to Ma Martha so she could put it in our piggy banks for a "rainy day". A day that never came.

Our final stop was the bakery for day old bread. I.E. always purchased two or three tall bags of bread. It wasn't just the bread that Little Bit and I was interested in. The bread was used to enrich the hog slop but there were treats as well. Mixed in the bags of bread we found cupcakes, pies, cookies or even whole cakes. Most of them were still in their wrappers and tasted as though they had just been baked. The cakes and pies were kept for Sunday's dessert; the cookies and cupcakes were snacks and weekday desserts.

Summers were pleasurable, I dreaded seeing them end. Boot camp was about to began. Aunt Dora a tall, thin, well poised, hard shelled school teacher lived in Greensboro, North Carolina which was too far for daily commute. She lived with us during school season. Her schoolhouse was a one room school that sat on the grounds of I.E.'s church. She was loved by all of the parents but many of the children were afraid of her. Her concern for Little Bit and me was often verbally expressed, but she gave us no breaks; not at home or in school. Before we were old enough to legally attend school, we were present more often than most of the registered students. We had to sit upright, walk right and God forbid if we mispronounced a word or used broken English. We were ordered to rewrite and pronounce that word over and over again. There were times when I got caught cheating by skipping numbers. I had to start over, doubling the starting number. She didn't care how long it took. If necessary she would send me to bed, only to start again the following day. I would purposely print slow or misspell a word, trying to wear her down but it never happened. An elbow on the table earned us a whack by her ruler; right on the "funny bone". It wasn't uncommon to hear her correcting I. E. and Ma Martha.

I was labeled by her as the "most stubborn, conniving child of all the world." That I was, and enjoyed every moment of being the devil's advocate. My witty personality enhanced my popularity among the students. I was being punished so frequently, lunch and recess often passed me by. One striking incident occurred on the morning when I wanted to stay home and sleep. I was made to go to school anyway. As I rode to school I promised myself that someone would pay for this dearly. "Oh yeah!, she will be sorry," I told myself.

Aunt Dora always arrived at least thirty minutes before the students. That was enough time for me to steal the chalk and hide it in my lunch box, with the intentions of throwing it in the toilet later. As she rang her hand held bell, warning everyone that class was about to begain, she walked to the blackboard to write her class assignments. Searching for a piece of chalk, she walked directly to my desk. I gave her a daring look, as to say , "find it if you can". She did. My punishment was to spend the day in the dark coat closet. She should have known better. I had just been handed the opportunity and the means to "compensate" her well. I wasn't tall enough to reach the string to pull the light on. I used the little light that gleamed through the cracks around the door to pull all the coats except mine to the floor, making sure that Aunt Dora's coat was on top. I urinated and defecated on them, using the sleeves of her wool coat to clean myself. I'm sure this was one of my better counteractions. To avoid further punishment for relieving myself I took a bite of my stolen "chocolate candy" to give myself diarrhea. I could get sick whenever I wanted to and I always wanted to when I was due for punishment. Being sick for a couple of days with some kind of "stomach virus" got me lots of rest. That's exactly what I was trying to get in the first place.

On Saturday evenings everyone knew to head over to Uncle Robert's and Aunt Mabel's to party. When sober Uncle Robert was quiet and easy going but he always talked as though he was inebriated. He was the neighborhood entertainer. His accident didn't stop him from getting his "tardy for his body", usually it was moonshine. They had an old organ and Uncle Robert would bang a few notes as he tried to sing some "down home blues." After a few more drinks he would start up the old phonograph and pull Aunt Mabel up and they would "shake a leg" the rest of the evening. These were the times when he really became talkative and slurred his speech even more. Throwing his head to one side, he started every sentence with, "lis-sen, hope got-may-kill-me."

Entertaining wasn't Uncle Robert's only specialty, he had a roving eye and hands alike. Taking chances he would invite his lady friend there among the other guest. Aunt Mabel wanted everyone to believe that she wasn't jealous but her actions said otherwise. She watched his every move. One afternoon after he had too much to drink, he grabbed his lady friend and told on himself. Dancing amorously, pinching the forbidden body parts, swearing what he was going do with "all this" started a one woman war. Everyone else must have known who this lady was. The expression on their faces told more than words could possibly say. Aunt Mabel made one move toward the woman; yelling a few curse words. The visitors scattered in every direction. The yard was emptied within seconds except the three and Aunt Mabel had both of them on the ground, beating first one then the other; cursing with every strike. The woman crawled from Aunt Mabel's clutches, then she got up and ran. Uncle Robert was too drunk to get away. When Aunt Mabel finished beating him she left him laying there.

Strong drinks or the "devil's music" was never allowed in our home. Ma Martha and I. E. never attended any of the shindigs.

They were too busy praying for the sinner's souls. Declaring, "all that mess is the work of the devil." Ma Martha constantly warned us. "You don't have to open a door for the devil to come in; he can slip through any crack." Little Bit and I only went over for a fish sandwich or hot dogs. If children were there we had to invite them over to our yard to play.

Sundays were sacred. Only the mandatory chores were done. This was a day for worship and rest. I. E. and Ma Martha were both of the Baptist faith but their memberships were in different churches. This did not cause a problem because the churches only held service one Sunday each month. Ma Martha's church; River Zion Baptist was every second Sunday and I.E.'s, Hammer Baptist was every third Sunday. First, fourth and fifth Sundays we visited other churches. All the churches had the same format and most of the same people were in attendance.

I. E. was the oldest member and head deacon in his church. He had a special chair in the amen corner. His church duties included praying, assisting with the devotions and overseeing the finances. His devotions stirred the spirit in the church. From his chair he'd start a song in words and the congregation joined in song, as he moved to the front of the church. A very familiar praise song was "Amazing Grace." He'd start it.

"Amazing Grace how sweet the sound, that saved a wretch like me."

The congregation would come behind him, slowly singing.

"A-maz-ing grace-how sweet the sound-That saved a wretch like me!"
He'd continue.

"I once was lost but now I'm found, was blind but now I see."
Again the congregation followed. By the second verse, praises were being expressed throughout the church. He was definitely the pillar of the church as well as Rev. Earl's confidant. Many church affairs were discussed and settled in our home.

Ma Martha held no documented position in her church but when she stepped in everyone acknowledged her. Just her appearance was a great honor. She had a "Holy look", a glow that could not be explained. Her hats and suits improved her million dollar walk. She never sought prestige or honor, nor did she try to impress anyone; she was just being herself; a straight forward no pretense kind of person.

My individualism in church became as antagonistic as at home. As I watched different ones jump and shout all over the church, I couldn't understand why I had to "sit still and listen" amid all the noise that they were making. We were taught to rejoice in the Lord always. Yet, I received one on my worst whipping when I "laughed and rejoiced" at an old ugly woman with torn cotton stockings and turned over shoes, shouting. Honestly, she looked like a clown that had escaped from a circus.

Church chastisement became so predictable it forced Ma Martha to carry a leather belt in her purse. She would take me outside and pull my dress over my head; there she had a "halleluiah" time beating my bottom. Matters were made worst when she would force me to apologize to my perpetrators. Before I fully understood the definition of apology I was compelled to apologize to a hideous church mother for losing her wig while shouting. I had never seen a wig before. I grabbed the hair and ran across the church. It was amazing to me. Instead of an explanation; we had our private meeting outside. I was further shocked when I was made to apologize. I thought the woman should have apologized to me. "She was the one who shouted out of her hair, it fell on us," I said. Nevertheless, I did as I was told. "I'm sorry mam that you're so ugly that your hair wouldn't stay on." I quickly realized that I had said something wrong when Ma Martha grabbed me by one arm and shoved me in the car. This time our private meeting was held at home.

Church was the only place where Ma Martha didn't complain about spending too much money. They both loved their church and their pastor. Every month their pastors had a standing invitation at our house to receive love gifts. We assembled each a box of vegetables, meats, canned goods, eggs, flour, meal and frozen butter. I. E. always met them at the door with folded money. Cheerfully reaching out to the pastors he'd say, "here's a little something, line your pockets." The pastors never counted the money. They accepted it as if it was to be a secret, quickly sliding it in their pockets.

There are two well known characteristics concerning southern preachers. They all have hefty appetites and they are always late. I chose to teach them a lesson about being on time. While I. E. and Ma Martha was sitting on the front porch waiting for their spiritual leaders, Little Bit and I were in the kitchen helping ourselves to dinner. By the time the pastors and their wives showed we had eaten the choice chicken parts, cut the ham from every angle; leaving mostly scraps, ate a whole sweet potato pie and drank most of the Kool-Aid. Rev. Wilson; Ma Martha's pastor cleared us of our wrong doings that time. I believe that Ma Martha was more embarrassed than she was angry. The wives helped to rearranged the table and everyone dined as though nothing had gone wrong. The most hilarious part was the blessing of the meal. I laughed when Rev. Wilson said, "Lord we thank You for the food that we're about to receive," I thought, "I thank You to, for the food that I've already received."

CHAPTER THREE

Being an inquisitive child, I questioned Daddy regularly concerning his whereabouts when his weekly visits became biweekly or even monthly despite the fact that he lived only a few miles down the road. His fabricated explanation was that his time was spent maintaining the family farm during the day and working in a tobacco factory at night. His visits were important to me because he always had something for us. He would also take us for a ride or visit other relatives.

Daddy had given up housekeeping after Mama's death and moved in with his parents. They were well up in age; grandma being much younger. My memory of grandpa is not that great. He was sickly and didn't live long after we started visiting them. His death occurred on one of our weekend visits. I was listening to the grown-ups conversation when I heard them saying that grandpa had been talking with his mother all that day. His mother had passed many years earlier. According to their knowledge of death and visits from "beyond" this was a sign that grandpa was dying and his mother had come for him. Whether their philosophy was accurate or not is still a mystery to me but about dusk that evening he passed. Prior to his passing the most ethereal scene occurred. This shocked everyone. A beautiful, blinding, "pearly white" light came through the house, briefly hovered over grandpa's bed, exited through the window and ascended into the heavens. According to the adults that ray of light was grandpa's vehicle to heaven.

From all of her pictures, grandma was a real eye catcher in her younger days. A tall, fair skinned woman with long "good hair". She often told us that she was part Indian. This stage in her life she had become a little hunchback, a goiter had grown on her throat but she didn't allow those miner frailties slow her dowm. She was always busy loving and caring for her grandchildren. Her nine children adored her as well as her name. There are four granddaughters named after her; me being one of them.

Weekends at grandma's meant freedom to do as we pleased. We listened to the radio station of our choice, watched television until it signed off. Most of all we didn't have to worry about getting up for church on Sunday mornings. We ate when and if we wanted to. Grandma made the best bologna sandwiches. She had that thick bologna and fried it before making the sandwich. Her banana sandwich was equally as tasty. To this day I still treat myself to these sandwiches, customizing them with slice tomatoes or cheese.

At last, I was old enough to start school legally. Fortunately for me I didn't have to attend Aunt Dora's school. The county had just opened regular schools throughout the county. We were assigned to New Dotmond, an elementary school approximately twenty miles from our house. This school had a cafeteria where we could purchase hot lunches, an auditorium for assemblies and dances. Though we had to keep the dances hushed at home, we did attend the socials. We were able to ride the school bus everyday, not just Friday afternoons when Aunt Dora went back to Grensboro. She was assigned to a different school; High Rock. She had teacher friends who would report on me as if they were paid informants. Also, a few of the teachers from my school were members of our churches and they would stop by with negative reports. My daily activites included fighting and disrespecting the teachers. Whatever the story was, the verdict was the same.

Everything in our household was done as a family. My punishment was no different. Punishment ceremonies were held at night, after dinner. I should say every night after dinner. I. E. did the praying and reading the scriptures. Ma Martha did the whipping. He read two scriptures from the book of Proverbs, "he that spareth his rod hateth his son," and "train up a child in the way he should go," so many times until I could have quoted them for him. Before Ma Martha started the thrashings she would have me undress, "so she wouldn't wear out my clothing," she never failed to mention how much she hated to do this. She'd declare, "you may not understand this now, but you will in a long run." I only wished that she could read my mind. I wanted to ask her to wait until the long run to whip me. I must say if whippings were any indication of love, the Saunders "literally" loved the "Hell" out of me.

Shopping for our clothing was Daddy's responsibility. Unless there was a special occasion and with the exception of Christmas, Daddy only took us shopping each season. We always had three groups of clothing; one for play, school and Sundays. I never had to worry about getting hand-me downs. I was the youngest, but I was the largest, so my "too small clothes" were handed-up to Little Bit. Everything came from Sears Roebuck & Company.

A strange feeling would always come over me every time we went shopping. Blacks were allowed to shop in the department stores but it was obvious that we weren't welcomed. One Fall season, Daddy sought the assistance of a reluctant white sales lady. "Good evening Madam, will you please help my girls pick out a few school outfits, a coat a piece and a couple of church dresses?"

The lady gazed at us as if we were a pile of dung. In a subtle dubious tone she asked, "did you say a few pieces?"

I suppose she was implying that we weren't allowed to have a change of clothes.

"Yes'um."

Daddy responded softly.

In between servicing her white customers she half-heartedly helped us. Her way of fitting us was holding a dress up against us; whereas her white customers were allowed to go in a fitting room. After making our selections Daddy stepped forward, often paying with all large bills. Suspiciously accepting the money, she examined each bill several times before placing them in the cash register. The clothing was loosely folded and thrown in a bag. Never a "thank you" or "come again" parted her lips.

Our shopping sprees were also bonding time. We often bonded over a meal. Like most children, we always chose hot dogs, hamburgers and French fries. Many of the cafeterias did not serve blacks so we made our table in the bed of the truck. Occasionally we were allowed to ride in the back of the truck.

In my second year of school my world was invaded again . I didn't want to believe my eyes the day our school bus rolled to a stop in front of our house. Daddy was standing by the roadside waiting to meet us. The same black hearse that took mama away was sitting in the yard near the front door. I didn't know that I.E.'s body was already in the hearse. We were taken to the back porch where Ma Martha was sitting. Heart broken and crying she hugged us as she gave us the bad news. "You two is all I have now. The Good Lord came by here today and took our I. E. home. He did pause to say 'good-bye' and he sent his love to you."

I didn't want to hear anymore. I broke loose from her and ran back to the front porch. As I sat on the edge of the porch crying, the mortician hung a wreath on the door and slowly drove away.

    I can vaguely remember I. E.'s funeral. I'm not sure if I have suppressed it unconsciously or not, I held a great deal of anger for a long time. I felt that I. E. knew what time we got in from school and he should have paused long enough to tell us good-bye before dying. I do know that the wake was held at his church and his body stayed in the church overnight, but I can't recall any of the preparations for the service at home.

    Quickly our home became a house; lonely and empty. As strong as Ma Martha was and as much faith as she possessed, her williness to fight started dwindling. Even so, she never stopped praying or singing. Early in the mornings or late at night she could be heard singing an old spiritual. A frequent one was "Walk With Me".

> Walk with me Lord, Lord walk with me
> Walk with me Lord, Lord walk with me
> All along my tedious journey,
> I want Jesus to walk with me.

So much pain could he heard in her voice as she continued.

> In my sorrow, Lord walk with me
> In my sorrow, Lord walk with me
> All along my tedious journey,
> I want Jesus to walk with me.

Following her song, she'd pray, first thanking God for being so good down through the years. Then confessing that her soul was tired and she was ready for her eternal rest. She never ended without praying for us, asking God to build a fence around us so the enemy couldn't harm or destroy us.

Our family outings were the only event in our lives that kept a little laughter and togetherness among us. I'm sure that she only continued the peddling trips for my sake. She knew that making money excited me. I always raced to make more.

Ma Martha never learned to drive. We took the mill bus to town every Wednesday. An old school bus had been painted red and it came around early on week days transporting the mill hands, but for twenty-five cent anyone could ride. It wasn't known if the bus was named after the man or the man nicked named after the bus. An obese white man name Red drove the bus. He was cordial and helpful. He'd struggle from the driver's seat and step down from the bus, often shaking Ma Martha's hand as he took the largest basket and ushered us to the rear of the bus.

Ma Martha tried to shield us from the segregation problems. She had a way of making things seem right no matter how amoral they were. We'd experienced the separation of color all of our young life. In our schools, churches, stores and the buses. As a child this bothered me. In the home we were taught that we are all God's children, yet, the world is separated. Something is wrong, I surmised.

In our immediate neighborhood everyone was friendly enough. On the edge of Uncle Robert's and Aunt Mabel's property line was a "white folk" church. The pastor invited us to attend their services. We never physically attended any of their services but we enjoyed many of their spring and summer revivals from our relative's yard. If there was a funeral at the church Aunt Mabel would walk to the edge of her garden to speak with the deceased's family members; offering her condolences but mainly she wanted to know the cause of death.

As we boarded the partially filled bus one Wednesday I took the front seat behind the driver. "I'm going to sit here where I can see," I yelled to Ma Martha. She came close to pulling my arm out of the socket as she dragged me to the back of the bus. Pouting, I asked, "why is it that we always have to sit back here? I can't see a thing."

Motherly, as usual she answered. "Honey, we have so much room back here. Space to relax without being rubbed against by the others getting on." I was slapped in the mouth when I noticed aloud that all the "white folks" didn't mind being rubbed against.

The very thing that she tried to protect us from brought her down. While in town one week we got caught between Civil Rights Demonstrators, fireman and police officers. The policemen and firemen were beating and practically drowning Blacks. Using the force of water they broke the human linked chain. One turned his hose on us. We were pushed to the ground. Grabbing us while on her knees, Ma Martha pleaded for our safety. "Please sir, please don't hurt my babies. We ain't bothering nobody. All we're trying to do is get to the bus station so we can go home."

A big foot white officer stood towering over us as we sat on the ground, soaking wet.

"You niggers ain't got no business in the street, I should drown your axxxx."

His words were so degrading and piercing. He lifted one foot and made a move as though he was going to stomp us. Instead he spat in Ma Martha's face. When we finally got to our feet, Ma Martha thanked the nefarious officer and we ran down the street to the bus station leaving our baskets behind.

Inside the "colored" rest room while wringing the water from our clothes, Ma Martha was able to thank God for His "goodness and mercy". I thought, "how can anyone see goodness and mercy in being dxxxxx near drowned by a group of white folks?' However, that was a thought that stayed in my head. I'm sure if I had voiced it, the punishment would have been worst than the near drowning.

This was our last family day in the city. We didn't get a chance to eat ice cream or count and separate our money, so this was my most profitable day.

Ma Martha's weariness began to show, as did her health. The only doctor in our area that made house calls made quite a few to our house. All the prayers, medications and doctoring could not rerout our family's destiny.

History kept repeating itself. We were getting off the school bus one afternoon, my heart rose to my throat when we saw Ma Martha lying on the porch. She had fallen from the swing while waiting for us to get in from school. Dropping my book bag, I ran to her while Little Bit ran to get Aunt Mabel. I called out to her but her response was near null. Her mouth had twisted and she had no use of her right side. Aunt Mabel had called the doctor before coming over. One look at Ma Martha, she made her diagnoses. "Ms Mart'a don' had uh strok'." Exactly what the doctor diagnosed as he summoned an ambulance.

Being hospitalized for a few weeks and regaining only a limited amount of speech Ma Martha gave up all will to fight. Her last request was to come home to get her business straight.

Sitting around her bedside was Uncle Robert, Aunt Mabel, a white couple from up the road and a lawyer as she made her will. It was established that Uncle Robert and Aunt Mabel would keep us until we got grown. Aunt Mabel assured her of that, acknowledging that "des chil'en will always have a home." "Da home plac' is dars, promised Aunt Mabel.

This was a moment of closure for Ma Martha. She beckoned for Little Bit and me to come to her bedside. As restricted as her speech was; she made it clear that she was going to heaven to live with I. E. and Mama. She requested a promise that we would live a life that will bring us to them. I made that guarantee but in my heart I was praying that she would stay here with us. Another unanswered prayer. She took her flight late that night.

Realizing how lonely Ma Martha was without I. E. and knowing that she didn't suffer for an extended period of time was a bit of consolation in her passing.

Ma Martha's "Home Going" was almost identical to Mama's. Her coffin sat in the hallway all night for viewing. She was dressed in all white with a Bible at her side. We were old enough to know that this wasn't good night, but good-bye.

CHAPTER FOUR

It was only a few days after Ma Martha's death when we realized that we were no longer wanted on the farm. Perhaps Aunt Mabel's promise to Ma Martha was to relieve a dying woman's mind. Maybe she was seeking special recognition from her "white" neighbors. Whatever the reason; she arrogantly approached Daddy at Ma Martha's repast; threatening to put the "law" on him if he didn't come and get us.

"My ner'es can't tak' ra'sing no chillens", she blurted out. Everyone who attended the repast clearly heard and saw her ramping and raving. "I ain't gonna ke'p des chillens. Da'll nev'a kill me. If you don't com' and get'em, I'll sho' 'nough call da law. You can b'leeve dat." Her actions shocked Uncle Robert. He just stood speechless and in dismay.

Aunt Dora couldn't take us because it would interfere with her teaching job. At least that was her excuse for not taking us. I'm sure that she had other motives. She was middle age, never been married or had children. She was not going to burden herself with us. Me especially, she didn't want.

Our move with Daddy was a tragedy. He'd moved from grandma's into a rented house a few miles up the road. It was off the highway, down a dirt road lined with pine trees. An old wooden house, but I really liked it. It had a porch similar to Ma Martha's; the length of the house. This one had two front entryways. "At last we have our separate bedrooms," I shouted.
"Not so fast young lady, I have a woman that's gonna move in with us," Daddy replied.
My mind started roaming. "A woman!, could we have a new mother?" My daydream was interrupted by the rattling noise of an old model car coming down our driveway.

What a let down that was. She couldn't be a mother. Actually, she wasn't much of a woman. A small, fragile looking old woman stepped from the car and headed toward the porch. Wearing her glasses low on her nose, she ordered Daddy and the man who drove her there to "fetch" her bags. I wondered how could Daddy do this to us? Without knowing her age, I was sure that she was right along there with the dirt that she walked on. At first I didn't care for the old lady and decided that I would drive her away. Daddy introduced her as "Cousin Irene". I informed him that he had found a "cousin's corpse". "It's just a matter of time before we'll be burying you," was my cynical hello. As Daddy was about to chastise me she stepped in. "Oh le've hu a-lone. I kin han'le hu." The old lady was full of spunk and yes, another prayer warrior. She wasted no time letting me know her position in the home. "I's da gro'n-up he'e. I's gonna tak' ca'e of yo'll and I's don't tol'rate no foolis'ness."

It wasn't too difficult for me to start respecting her. In a peculiar sort of way I grew to love the old lady. We found out later that she was a blood cousin but that didn't matter because in the South everybody is everybody's cousin, uncle or aunt.

Cousin Irene had never gone to school but she showed concern about our schooling. On school nights we were in the bed no later than eight-thirty. Before sending us off in the mornings she made sure that we had prayer and a hot breakfast. Her medical advice became redundant. "Ya can't le'rn a thang on uh em'ty stomic."

After school we couldn't play until we had a snack and completed all homework. Hearing her set of laws caused me to visualize my extra playtime. "A lady that can't read or write; she won't know if my homework is done or not." I pondered within. I got away with it for a while, until there came a day when I became a little too eager to play. I told her that arithmetic was my only assignment and I had finished that. Of all the days, she chose to look over my work. Even then I wasn't worried until she solicited Little Bit's help.

"Lo'k a heea Lit'le Bit. Go ov'a yo sus'tas pap'a. Uh fine p'ece of wo'k he'e." Little Bit immediately realized that I had only copied the math problems. I had not solved any of them. Little Bit explained this to Cousin Irene. Thinking fast, I produced a hasty explanation. Innocently I explained. "My teacher told us to do this page, she never said anything about solving them." Cousin Irene may have had great discernment of the Holy Spirit, but she had no perceptiveness of children's schemes. She accepted my lie. "Well ba'be, I's sho' she wan'ed ya to 'plain wha' dis is. En'e how ya do it, and sho' hu how sma't ya is." I was delighted just to acknowledge my "misunderstanding."

Daddy was an excellent provider and a hard worker. His work week started Sunday midnight where he worked in a tobacco factory on the outskirts of Danville, Virginia. Arriving home in the morning he'd go to work on the farm, which was located down grandmas'. Often he'd bring water from grandma's well, if not he would get it from the near-by spring. He didn't allow Cousin Irene to do any heavy chores. Getting only a few hours of sleep; he would repeat his schedule through Thursday night. If he didn't have any farm work on Friday morning he would grocery shop before coming home. Whether he shopped in route or later that day, never a week passed when he didn't restock the cabinets and freezer. Before going to bed he made sure that there was enough wood cut for the following week.

With all the house work and field work done, he had the weekend to rest for the week to come. Not so, his heart was set elsewhere. I soon realized that all the weekends that he didn't spend with us while we were up Ma Martha's were spent with his drinking buddies. It was a great disappointment to find out that my daddy was a weekend alcoholic. He would leave home on Friday evenings; coming back on Sunday, usually so drunk he could hardly stand upright. It didn't seem possible that this was the same gentle and caring man whom I knew when Mama was alive. Yet, the most mind-boggling thing was that he could go all week with liquor in the house and he never touched it. When he should have been home for family time, he didn't recognize our existence. I refused to accept this. Animosity began to fester in me. I remembered Ma Martha's sayings about strong drinks and how the devil worked through it. I went to his private stock and poured it out. I swore that I would never allow any more liquor in our home.

Cousin Irene was blamed for throwing his liquor away. Stumbling in before dawn the next Sunday morning he was irritated and decided to start an argument. Cousin Irene never argued, instead she prayed. When he heard her praying he got his shot gun and started shooting around her feet as he yelled. "Where is your God now?"

She danced around the floor, dodging bullets and crying out to God. "Lo'd how mucy on dis man. He'p h'm Lo'd."

He mouthed back at her.

"He'd better help you, 'cause I'm gonna kill you this morning."

Suddenly the shooting stopped. He must have run out of bullets but he was still cursing and threatening her life.

Laying in our bed in the next room I had heard more than I cared to. I made up my mind that I will have to kill him this day. I waited for him to go upstairs to his room. Cousin Irene was sitting in her room praying and thanking God for sparing her life. When I heard him snoring I tipped upstairs. Using a kerosene lamp which we kept full in case the lights went out, as they often did during a storm, I poured kerosene on his bed linen and threw a match on it. Knowing that Little Bit and Cousin Irene was down stairs and could get away safely I ran down stairs screaming, "Get out! Get out quick, I've set his bed on fire! I've burned the devil up!" Daddy could be heard cursing as he fought the flames. Cousin Irene grabbed two buckets of water from the kitchen and went up to help him. From the bottom of the stairs, I yelled out to him.

"You're just lying on her. She didn't do it, I did it, and I'll do it again! I will burn you down!"

He was still cursing, now he was promising to kill me. Little Bit and I ran several miles in the early morning hours, through the woods for fear that he might come up the highway looking for us. We were scarcely dressed and by the time we reached Uncle Robert's and Aunt Mabel's house we were covered with brier pricks, scratches and chiggers.

Uncle Robert heard our knocks and cries for help. Pulling his denim overalls up as he opened the back door he asked, "lis'n, what's da mat'er wit' yo'll?"

Still crying I told him the story. Aunt Mabel heard us from her bedroom and came running in the kitchen and asked. "You done burn up yo' ho'se?"

"I don't know, they were trying to put it out when we left." I cried. Uncle Robert ordered Aunt Mabel back to the bedroom. " Lis'n Mabel, go cal' da law. Tel'm to me't us dar. Hope-got-may kil-me, I'm gonna kil' me a nxxxxx dis mo'ning." He swore. "I ain't sca'ed of no-body."

Uncle Robert slipped his feet in his boots; Aunt Mabel pulled a dress over her night gown. As we started out Uncle Robert grabbed his shotgun.

Aunt Mabel pleaded, "Robe't, don cha ta'e dat gun, you know da law gonna be dare."

Uncle Robert snapped back. "Lis'n, wom'n geet outta my way. I don to'd ya, I ain't sca'ed of da law. Let somebody mess wit' me or dees sheer chillens, hope-got-may kil'-me, I'll shoot'em de'd in his axx" Sure enough we rode down the road in the company of his shotgun.

We reached our house before the sheriff. It was now completely daylight. Fortunately for us only the mattress and the bed were destroyed. Daddy and Cousin Irene were throwing pieces of the charred bed out of the window. Aunt Mabel went in with us. She was the family mouthpiece and mastermind. Uncle Robert stayed in the car with his body guard. She forcefully called out to Daddy.

Lloyd, geet yo' axx down he'e, da law's on da way. yo axx's go'n to ja'l dis mo'ning."

Cousin Irene rushed down to quieten Aunt Mabel.

Our county had only one sheriff; a pudgy middle age white man with an unimpressive reputation of his own. The word around the county was that Bernie Smith was totally illiterate. People were saying that he had his arrestees writing their own tickets and summons. Stories were also being told of cases that had to be thrown out of court because of all the flawed information that his detainees had written; some allegedly wrote "Bernie Smith" as the defendant. I don't know the worthiness of all the stories but I do know that Uncle Robert was stopped for driving under the influence many times and he couldn't write either. He never receive a written ticket. The sheriff would tell Uncle Robert to meet him Monday morning at the courthouse. It was then when Uncle Robert was officially charged and fined; through the court. Uncle Robert never ventured too far from home when he was out socializing. His mistress lived only a mile or so down the road. When he was stopped by Mr. Smith the degree of his drunkenness determined his way home. If he was sloppy drunk, the sheriff would drive him home; otherwise he would follow Uncle Robert; either way Aunt Mabel was instructed to hold the keys until Monday. One thing Mr. Smith was credited for was his good memory. It was said that he never missed a court date or got his charges mixed up.

I was hoping that the sheriff would hurry to our house. Daddy and Aunt Mabel shared no lost love and they would be at each other's throats in a matter of minutes. Cousin Irene knew this and offered to wait for the sheriff on the porch with her. Aunt Mabel rejected her offer. "Hell no, I won'em to brang his sor'y axx do'n he'e." Aunt Mabel was about to go upstairs after him when the sheriff walked through the door. Seeing the bullet holes in the floor, the sheriff immediately called Daddy down and asked only one question.

"Did you do this boy?"

Daddy nodded and replied, "yes sir."

He was taken off to jail.

Everyone knew grandpa and all of his children. The family name and the attorney that Daddy could afford changed the whole story. He was released on his own recognizance and back home before the dust could settle.

This episode gave us a few weeks of peace and harmony in the home while waiting for his trial. Daddy went out of his way to keep us happy. Cousin Irene swallowed it all. Somehow I knew that this was all a smoke screen that he and his illusive lawyer had arranged. I tried to get Cousin Irene to see it but she was too busy thanking God for the great change. She constantly made her anticipation known.

"Hush chi'd, ya dad'y 's gonna be jes' fin'."

Daddy was so careful in his deceptions that he joined in and even led some of the meal prayers. We were taken to town to shop for new outfits for the trial. He purchased himself a new suit. Oh no, he was too smart to say that we were shopping for the trial. However, on the morning that we were due in court he rushed in from his night job and instructed us to put on our "new" Sunday best.

We walked in the courthouse behind Daddy and his attorney; sashayed down the aisle as though as we owned the place. They saw us to the first bench as they strutted up to the defendant's table. That's where they sold the story to the judge.

It worked. "A hard working young widower, father of two beautiful little girls with a hired nanny to care for them," was the opening scene. This was also when I learned that Cousin Irene was a "hired nanny."

Cousin Irene fell further into their trap when the judge asked her if the family differences had been reconciled. She eagerly stood and without a clear understanding of what the judge was asking, she made her statement.

"Well sur, I 'pose you's as'en if eve'y thang's alrit. If dats so, ye'sur, swe't as ah ros' sur. Dat man don made a comp'ete tu'n 'round sur."

The judge found her to be amusing but he maintained his professionalism.

Daddy's punishment was only six months probation after his legal representative convinced the judge that he was shooting to scare us because he was afraid of an old woman and two small children so much so that he had his shotgun for self protection. One thing that worked in my favor was that he took the fire incident on himself; stating that he was smoking in bed.

Returning home was like heaven to us. We did things as a family. If Daddy went out on the weekends he would come home every night at a decent hour. There were times when I smelled liquor on his breath but he wasn't violent. He would sleep it off and the next morning at the breakfast table we would make family plans for the day. Many times we just stayed home and enjoyed each other's company which was alright with me.

The more I desired to hold on to this ephemeral dream the more it just ripped through my fragile heart. I had such an inexplicable insight. "All this will disintegrate any day." I told myself as I started counting the months, then days when Daddy's probation period would come to an end. So many times I had an urge to share my feelings with him. I wanted him to know that this "changed life" was the way that we should live always, but I never gained the courage to confront him.

I often think of the harmonious days with I. E. and Ma Martha. I envisioned the winter nights when I.E. would make a fire in the fireplace, together we popped popcorn, roasted peanuts or marshmallows. Sometimes Ma Martha would treat us to her delicious apple, cherry, sweet potato, or peach turnovers. Their reprimands and whippings were done in Christian love. I never thought that I'd be able to say this, but how I would welcome a whipping from her now. Maybe this was what Ma Martha meant when she said, "you'll understand in a long run." In fact I've held many conversations with her in the spirit whenever I felt the need for encouragement. I remember telling her how much I enjoyed and missed our "happy" meals. With a repentant heart I compassionately expressed my many past dislikes to her. "In times of yore I felt that you were punishing us for some unknown reason when you started us doing laborious duties around the house, like emptying and cleaning our personal bedside chamber pot, milking the cows, feeding the hogs and chickens before school. When we no longer woke up on Saturdays for a game of hopscotch; instead we had to heat water in a cast iron pot; so that we could wash clothes in the old wringer washing machine. Before we could rest for the day we had to scrub and disinfect the outside toilet. But you know Ma Martha, I would give anything to have that life back." She always responded. Such a calmness would rest upon me after my talks with her. I felt as though she was embracing me. Even in her death she made everything seem so right.

I often wondered if Daddy loved us at all. Could it be that he didn't won't to face his responsibilities? Every payday he gave us allowances, even more to spend as we wished. We always had money in our pockets, sometimes more than the adults. I have gone to school with as much as six hundred dollars in my pocket. Uncle Robert and Aunt Mabel gave us money as well. Especially during crop selling time, she would meet our school bus or send it by family members. If the tobacco sales were really great and our profits were large, she would bring it herself. Acknowledging, "dis is da mon'y from da 'bacco on you'll's lan'."

As much as I pretended in my childhood wealth, I was never really happy. What good was my money when I couldn't buy love?

A few months beyond Daddy's probation period, our family life came to an abrupt end. I felt that we were a cursed family and God didn't care to help. Our last weekend as a family ended one Saturday. Daddy came in with lots of groceries. He was in a good mood, even played dodge ball with us. Cousin Irene was baking pies and cakes to take to church the following day. The smells drove Daddy to rave about how good they must taste. He invited himself to church. "I believe I'll go with you all tomorrow. Yeah, I'm going to be there feasting with the good church folks."
"RING!"
My inner bell started ringing.
Cousin Irene broke out in a Holy dance, praising God.
"Tha'k ya Jes's. Lo'd, I'd alwa's bel'ed dat ya wa gonna cle'n dis man up. He cou'd be suc' a good man, ev'n a de'con in ya chu'ch. She went on and on, praising God for touching his heart and

Daddy for deciding to go with us. Around six o'clock that evening Daddy went out.

Sunday morning came; Daddy was no where to be found. Cousin Irene and Little Bit was busy in the kitchen preparing breakfast and packing her baskets to take to church.

The enemy finally appeared. Staggering through the front door, he made his way to the kitchen swearing every step of the way. "Ain't nobody going to church today. That dxxx judge just oughta had sent me to jail. You can tell the good preacher this." Without realizing that the house protector was behind him, he went face forward, barely missing the hot cook-stove when I kicked him in the back of his wobbly legs. Seeing a skillet of chicken frying, I yelled to Little Bit, "Throw the chicken on him!"
Cousin Irene grabbed her.
"Oh my God chi'd, don cha do dat! Dat hot gre'se 'll kil'im.
"That's what I want to do." I shouted as I grabbed our baseball bat from beside the water stand. I walloped his head as hard as I possibly could. Not sure what was going to happen next, I ran outside still dragging the bat.

Bleeding and practically crawling, Daddy came after me. Outside I jumped him again, vowing to kill him with every blow. I was pulled away by Cousin Irene.
"Lo'd how mu'cy chi'd, you don kilt ya da'dy."

Angry and sure that he was dead, I confirmed it. "Yes I did!, I killed him! I killed him grave yard dead!"

Daddy was stretched out, motionless, face down in the yard; bleeding from his head and God knows where else. Cousin Irene sadly took a seat on the porch and started praying. Little Bit and I ran up the road to call the sheriff again.

Returning with Uncle Robert and Aunt Mabel, seeing that nothing had changed, Aunt Mabel stepped out of the car waving her arms and blaring. "I know'd it. I know'd it. I know'd som'em lik' dis tas bound to hap'en." She walked on the porch and took a seat, still conversing with herself. "O'ly thang I kin sa' is he bout dis on his sef. He had no bus'nes mess'n wit dat chi'd. Well, he's a de'd axx now"

I suppose she was building me a self defense case. Uncle Robert never said a word; just took a seat and lit a cigarette. Little Bit and I stood by the car. She appeared to be frightened but I was too angry to be fearful.

Speeding down the driveway, leaving a trail of dust behind, the sheriff came to a screeching halt behind Uncle Robert's car. He pulled himself from his patrol car, threw his hat on his head as he walked toward the house. "What is it this time, Irene? From the looks of things here, you all done called the wrong man. Get me a sheet so I can cover this, while I 'vestigate what done happened here."

The sheriff, as did everyone else, assumed that Daddy was dead. He never checked for a pulse. The Lord came through for Cousin Irene. She bellowed , "HAL-LE-LU-JAH!!" Daddy moved trying to roll over when the sheriff attempted to cover him as if he was a cadaver. Sheriff Smith helped Daddy roll over by pushing him with his foot.

I don't know if Daddy went to the doctor or not because Aunt Mabel gathered a few of our clothes and took us to their house. Before leaving she made sure that Daddy knew that he got just what he deserved. "Y'u low do'n sca'dal. She shu'da kill'd yo sor'y axx Y'u too sor'y to la' do'n and die."
Daddy never responded. As we drove away he was sitting up on the ground and Cousin Irene was doctoring on his head. The sheriff was standing over them. No one went to church that Sunday.

Monday morning was a school day and Little Bit and I weren't sure if we were going or not. Aunt Mabel was sure, she got us ready and ordered us out to the roadside. She flagged down the first "colored folk" school bus that came along. Her main concern was to see if the bus was going to New Dotmond. The other concern was to make sure that she got the news out. I was overjoyed to hear that the first bus was going to our school, when

Aunt Mabel queried the driver.

"Go'd mon'n! Is dis shere bus go'ng to dat Dot'mon sc'ol?"

The young lady, a high school senior responded.

"Yes mam."

Instead of her allowing us on the bus, Aunt Mabel stepped on the first step and gave an in-depth version of why we were at her house.

"Des chil'ens'll be get'en on and off at my ho'se. Dat dad'y of dar's jus' ain't no blam' go'd. Da cant sta' wit'em no mo'. Dis chi'd (pointing to me) prut ne'r kil'ed 'im yesteedy."

A few of the children started laughing at her but the majority of them showed compassion as we got on and took our seats.

These living arrangements were short lived with very few admirable moments. We lived like guest in their house. I can't recall Aunt Mabel ever hugging us. Uncle Robert did when he was promising to protect us. "Lis'n, hope-got-may kill me. If any body mes' wit yo'll let me kno. Hope-got-may kill me, if I can't beat'm, I'l sho't'm."

I'll never forget the whipping that Aunt Mabel put on me unjustly. Little Bit and I was arguing one day; I told her that she was trying to be so "biggity", meaning impudent. Aunt Mabel swore that I called Little Bit a female dog, a word that I didn't know at that time. She whipped me unmercifully.

In late November 1963 our problems became so microscopic.

"Disappointment!"

"Heartaches!"

"Prayers!"

This all became a "Country Thing."

The news of President Kennedy's Assassination was spreading throughout the school. Teachers and students were crying. Some classrooms; mine included were equipped with televisions, this allowed us to follow the news all day.

The bus ride home was in total silence; everyone was grieving. When we reached our stop we saw Aunt Mabel in the yard waiting for us. Little Bit and I ran to break the news because she rarely listened to the radio and didn't turn the television on until after dinner. Before we could share the Nation's News she greeted us. Not a hello or how was school; she whooped. "Yo'll com' on he'e. I'm gonna sen' you'll up younda to Was'ing'on to liv' wit yo mama's sista. Da ain't nev'r don' not'en fo' yo'll, ain't se'n ya sinc' ya mammy di'd. We gonna go do'n to yo'lls ho'se to geet da res' of yo clo'hs."

Without taking a breath she yelled an order to Uncle Robert.

"Com'on he'e Robe't. Run us do'n da ro'd."

Nearing our house eased my anxious spirit. I knew that we would never call this place home again. I just wanted to end it and move on.

Daddy was home busy stacking firewood on the porch. He was surprised yet seemed happy to see us. I imagined he thought that we were coming back home. He was sober and extremely polite. His idiosyncrasy only ignited Aunt Mabel's rage. I believe Aunt Mabel was caught off guard. She wasn't expecting him to be home, but she didn't take down. She walked in front of him shaking one finger in his face. "I ain't com' do'n he'e fo' no blam' mes'. I'm sen'ing des chil'en to Was'ing'on dis even'in."
Daddy never raised his voice as he pleaded with her. "Ms Mabel, will you please stay out of my business?"
He was about to say something else but wasn't allowed.
"Y'u ain't got no dxxx bus'nes'." Aunt Mabel cursed him with all her might.

Cousin Irene was still there and apparently waiting for our return also. She came out and tried to settle all the animosity.
"Now all dis fus'ing and cus'ing do't mak'no se'se. Dees shere chil'en's ol' 'nough to 'cide fo' demself."
As intimidating as Aunt Mabel was, she made an ethical attempt to respect her elders.
"Now Mis' 'rene, dis ain't no co'cern of yo's. Y'u just gon' bac' in da ho'se."
"Yo'll chil'ens geet in dare and geet yo' thangs toge'er," she said

without missing a beat. Uncle Robert stayed in the car, door open, smoking a cigarette.

As we cleared our dresser drawers Little Bit stated wasn't sure if she wanted to move. She had become attached few friends and developed a childhood crush on one of her schoolmates. I reminded her that I had to do all the fighting. She or Cousin Irene wouldn't help me. "I'm not fighting anymore," I assured her. Aunt Mabel had said this was it for her as well.

Daddy slowly walked in our room, full of sorrow he questioned us. "Do you all know what you're doing? Is leaving here what you really want to do?" After a few seconds of silence and thinking on what I had just told Little Bit, I blurted out. "We want to go to Washington." Speechless and exhibiting great pain Daddy walked out of the room. Stronger than before, desires to hug Daddy engulfed me. I wanted him to know how much we loved him and wanted him to be a part of our lives, but as the previous times I did not act upon my feelings.

Uncle Robert started piling our belongings in the car. Cousin Irene came out to the car to pray with us, only to be interrupted by Aunt Mabel. "We ain't got no tim' fo' all dat. Yo'll geet in da car, y'u gotta geet to da bus sta'ion."
As we headed out I watched Daddy standing in the doorway until he was out of sight. Not even a simple goodbye.

Rushing back up the highway to finish packing was an understatement. Sending us to Washington must have been a last minute brainstorm of Aunt Mabel. She hadn't planned anything. Our suitcases were something that had been thrown back in her storage bin. They were old and dirty with layers peeling off and broken locks that had to be held together with assorted ropes and belts. Arrangements with our aunt in Washington were made when she called Little Bit in her bedroom to make the call.

"Com' he'e Lit'le Bit, you mak' dis shere cal'. You's ol' 'nough to lo'k afta you'll now."

Little Bit was so nervous, she was trembling as she dialed the operator for assistance. Getting through, and in tears, Little Bit made her request. "May I speak with Aunt Sally please?"

Aunt Sally must have answered. Little Bit continued. "Aunt Sally, can, can we.?" Before she could say another word, Aunt Mabel yanked the phone. "Can hell, Sal'y dis is Mabel. I's put'en dees shere chil'ens on da nex' bus to Was'ing'on. Y'u ca' pic'em up early in da mo'ning."

She hung up before getting an answer or telling her which bus we would be on. More upsetting, she handed us each a half sheet of lined notebook paper and told us to write our names and Aunt Sally's phone number on it. She pinned it to our coats with large diaper pins as if we weren't old enough to speak for ourselves.

Filling her lower lip with snuff and spiting across the room as she spoke, Aunt Mabel ordered us back in the car and Uncle Robert to load all our suitcases.

Grabbing our packed lunches from the table as we walked through the kitchen, we headed out the back door and left for the bus station.

I felt so empty. I wanted to cry, but I wasn't sure why. I was sure that there had to be a better life for us somewhere. I had the same feeling that I had when we were headed for the cemetery to bury both Mama and Ma Martha. Now, we were not headed for the burial ground but I was burying my past. I glanced toward the sky as we journeyed along. I couldn't see either mama. I felt that we were being thrown out here in this world all alone. Hardly any conversation was being shared.

Neither of my mama's were visible but their presence came through. It wasn't long before my pains and worries ceased. A quietness surrounded me. I was aware that I was sitting in a car riding, yet, I was taken up out of myself. I heard myself singing, though my lips were not moving. My soul was praying to God through song.

> "Pass me not O gen-tle Sav-ior, Hear my hum-ble cry, While on oth-ers Thou art call-ing, Do not pass me by.
> Sav-ior, Sav-ior, Hear my hum-ble cry,
> While on oth-ers Thou art call-ing, Do not pass me by.

Thou the Spring of all my com-fort, More than life to me, Whom have I on earth be-side Thee? Whom in heav'n but Thee? Sav-ior, Sav-ior, Hear my hum-ble cry, While on others Thou art call-ing, Do not pass me by."

Fanny J. Crosby

I was reminded of one of Ma Martha's sayings. "Only God can heal your wounded spirit."

When we reached the bus station Aunt Mabel made a dash for the door. Ignoring the people in line, she stomped right up to the counter. Without being acknowledged she demanded,
"t'o chil'en tic'ets to Was'ing'on."
The attendants looked at each other in disbelief; as did the people in line. They protested among themselves. Finally one associate shrugged her shoulders and agreed to serve Aunt Mabel to get rid of her. Little did she know; it wasn't that easy, as she inquired, "DC or State?"
"Sta'e what?" Aunt Mabel asked.
Irritated, the associate questioned her.
"Ms, which Washington do you want?"
"Da one up yonda by Bal'i'mo' Mar'lan'." Aunt Mabel responded as if the clerk was the ignorant one. She also seized that moment to vociferously inform all the travelers of our situation and why we

were being sent to Washington. She took her one woman show on the outside. As we were boarding the bus, she performed.

"Now you'll ain't got not'in to be sca'ed of.
Wh'n yo'll geet up yonda ya a'nt gonna geet ya. Now, it tis uh big plac', wit lots of fo'ks and plen'y of bri't ligh's. But lon' as Sal'y be'n dare, purt'n near 'nybody can po'nt ya to ha."
The bus driver constantly checked his watch and cleared his throat, trying to get her attention; which she completely ignored. She instructed us to call her as soon as we got to Sally's and write as often as we liked to let her know how we were doing.

Finally she turned to the driver and demanded that he look after us. She did not forgo her Southern hospitality.
"I don' fri'd uh whol' chic'en, so he'p yo se'f to uh san'wich. Dar's plen'y food in dare bags, y'u jus' let dem buy a soda pop at one of yo stops. Da got dar' o'n mon'y." The driver thanked her for the offer and gladly promised that he would watch out for us.

As soon as the bus left the station Little Bit and I looked at each other; reading the other's mind, we ripped the revolting name tags from our coats.

We started jumping up at every stop, looking for bright lights and lots of people. The bus was stopping at every nook and hole along the highway. It was dark and only one or two persons would alight or get on.

Little Bit and I started conversing about our expectations in the big city. We both hoped for a happy home life but more important Little Bit wanted to drop her nickname. A name which was fitting when she was young. Now a teen, she feels that she has outgrown it. She made me promise never to use her nickname again. "Ok". I agreed. "I will introduce you as Beth, but I will still use Dee, just one Dee though." We shook on it.

Finally at a city stop the bus driver came and asked if we were ready for a soda. We each gave him a dollar and our choice of soda. When he returned with our sodas he gave us our dollars back. "This is on me," he said. We thanked him. I offered him a piece of chicken but he refused.

"Sir how much farther do we have to go to get to Washington?" I inquired. He laughed, then said, "we yet have a ways to go, we're now in Richmond, Virginia, this is a thirty minute rest stop." Again, I thanked him for the information. Beth and I ate, drank our sodas, then went to sleep.

We were sitting midway the bus. Sometime about daybreak we were awaken by the driver. "Alright girls, this is your stop." Clearing the sleep from my eyes, I was flabbergasted. Sure enough there were people everywhere. The lights were brighter than the County Fair.

Stepping from the Greyhound we walked into the station.

Aunt Sally wasn't there, or anyone who appeared to be looking for someone. We were two young country girls lost in a big city. I became frightened and felt the need to care for my big sister. Surrounded by so many strange people, Aunt Mabel's "words of wisdom" came to mind. I walked through the bus station asking anyone who would stop to listen, "Do you know our Aunt Sally?" We had not a clue of her last name, not that it would have mattered.

Embarrassed by my actions Beth walked a few steps ahead of me, only stopping to plead with me. "Will you please stop making a fool of yourself. These people don't know who you're talking about."

To our benefit both bus stations were on the same street, just opposite each other. We were rescued when a short, shapely lady in a nurse's uniform and her husband, Uncle Paul, a tall well built man greeted us. Aunt Sally's first words were, "here you are, I would have known you anywhere." Pointing to me, " you're Dee Dee, you look just like your mother, my sister. Beth, you're the spitting image of your father." After all the hugs and greetings we went to claim our shoddy looking luggage. Getting everything loaded in their sparkling new cherry red and black Chevy we left for our new home.

It was boisterously entertaining mocking Aunt Mabel's

preconception of Washington and me being gullible enough to follow her commands.

Like North Carolina, Washington was mourning the President's death. The whole country was in grief. The White House was only a couple of blocks from the bus stations. We took a tour of downtown, around by Capitol Hill and Union Station before going home.

CHAPTER FIVE

The transition to the big city was indeed a dream come true. My dreams began to manifest themselves faster than I could comprehend. Home was a large three-story row house in Northeast, just blocks from the National Arboretum. A great deal of my free time was spent there admiring Mother Nature and meditating. I often compared my life to the life of the flowers and foliage as well as to a Scripture from the Bible that I'd heard often.

"My days are like a shadow that declineth; and I am withered like grass."
Psalms 102:11

I. E. quoted that scripture frequently, especially in his latter days. I suppose my thoughts on life have always been beyond my years. I'd always known that I was born for a reason and have a specific vocation here on earth. As the flowers that blossom we have only a season, then we will wither and die. I was determined not to allow pain and sorrow to be my only gain in "my season."

Sally, she allowed us to call her, worked many double shifts, often getting home near midnight. Uncle Paul took pleasure in his social life, going out after work at least three times per week, coming in late.

Their family consisted of a daughter one year older than me, a five-year-old son and a female cousin three years younger than me. A household of four girls either at or approaching adolescence with sundry minds must have tested Sally's sanity.

Life was finally taking a turn in my favor. A few friends, parties, movies, McDonalds, live shows at the Howard Theater and fun around the house. What more could any young American teenager hope for? This was certainly more than what North Carolina had to offer. I felt good about the fact that I didn't have to push the motherly persona anymore. No more fights to protect my big sister. She was still smaller than me.

Without delay Sally enrolled us in school. Aunt Dora's vigorous techniques must have paid off, I skipped a grade. We both started Browne Junior High School. The schools in Washington were much larger and more sophisticated than what I had been accustomed to. No longer the walk up or down the hall to a class; instead, up and down three floors to class rooms. Students were too numerous to recall from one class to another. Right away, I knew that I would never have the close knit school environment that I had left behind.

Junior High definitely had its prominence. Of all of my classes I was drawn to music the most. I'd always been a lover of music; I yearned to sing and play an instrument. I had no rhythm and couldn't hold a note if I could have held it in my hand. However, I did learn a few notes in North Carolina when I played the "tonette". It is the toy instrument in the clarinet family. I made appearances in school assemblies and 4-H Club programs. Twinkle, Twinkle Little Star and Row Your Boat was the extent of my musical performances. All of my singing was done in choruses where my voice couldn't be singled out. I decided to take a music class with the hopes of following my dream. It was far beyond my imagination when I was told that the renowned, Ms Roberta Flack would be my music instructor and homeroom teacher. Students would come in early and rush to homeroom where Ms Flack would be sitting at the piano playing and singing as if we were a paying audience. A petite, compassionate lady that could open her mouth and melodies would come rolling straight from the depths of her soul. She also performed locally at a super club. A few of us students were asked out of the club several times for trying to take in her performances. If she ratted on us or not, we never knew.

It was in my music class when I decided that music wasn't for me after all. Ms Flack's warmth and sensitivity did not stop her from asking me to put an exam paper in the trash can, acknowledging that she'd caught me cheating. I was too mortified to try to defend myself. I can honestly say, I have never cheated since then. I did pass her class with a "C" and that was a struggle.

Years started flying by as days. Sally decided that we had too much freedom and not enough supervision. She cut her workload and became the neighborhood mom. Our house served as the "clubhouse" for a youth group; "Young Leaders Of Tomorrow." Our uniforms were blue jeans with light blue blouses or shirts sporting the letters Y. L. O. T. across the back. Fundraisers were activated to defray our recreation expenses. Several trips per summer to various amusement parks kept us entertained. Meetings were held weekly, ending with rap sessions and refreshments. Everyone, especially the girls found it easy to talk with Sally. She was the unofficial neighborhood counselor as well. The guys were reluctant to talk about sex or becoming an adult. This did not discourage Sally. Her charm could get a stone to converse with her. Sally was not compensated monetarily for her services but was honored with certificates and plaques from the city. Her greatest reward was being a part of our lives; not just us in the home but the young girls and guys in the neighborhood as well.

House parties were another method for Sally to keep an eye

on us. Once each month the club members were allowed to have a house party as long as we obeyed her strong demands. Sally's five "NO" laws.

No music after one a.m.

No intoxicating beverages.

No loud noise or hanging around outside the house.

No profanity or disrespect of any kind.

No member was to leave until everything was clean and furniture back in place." Following Sally's demands was a pleasure; there was never a problem.

It was the club parties that produced a fruitful relationship for me. A neighbor and classmate had told me that her cousin had seen me and wanted to get to know me. One momentous night that will forever be dear in my heart; she invited him to the party. Lewis was a medical student and local entertainer. He was the perfect "prescription" for me. Working part time at a local hospital left little time for us because most of his weekends were spent either working or doing gigs. Without Sally's knowledge I attended many of Lewis's performances. I don't know why I kept going because time and time again I came home sad and bursting with insecurities. Watching the countless screaming and salivating young ladies grabbing after him as he performed crushed my heart. He must have sensed my feelings. He sealed our love the night that he walked off stage, with his eyes fixed on me, he sang his way to my seat, took my hand and publicly serenaded me. Tears of joy met under my chin. I knew that we were predestined to be together. I also knew that I had to keep his age classified. Lewis was nine years older than me. Sally and Uncle Paul would have never stood for that.

Uncle Paul gave Sally full range of overseeing our social life. He never participated in any of our club arrangements. However, he did reprimand us in the home. His punishments could be rather harsh at times. Coming home in the wee hours he expected the house to be immaculate at all times. If he found a glass in the sink or the pillows on the couch out of place, he'd get all of us up and make us clean the whole first floor, even polishing the hardwood floors. His punishments also became my avenue for revenge. If I had a dispute with anyone in the house, I settled it by leaving a dish in the sink or making the front room untidy; punishing everyone, including myself.

Church was not forced upon us and we weren't searching for it either. Sally's work schedule dictated her church capabilities. She did make many attempts to persuade us to go. There was a church on nearly every street corner. We really didn't have any good excuses why we wouldn't go other than we just didn't want to go. Several ministers were called to conduct Bible study in the home. That soon fizzled out to. I felt that I'd heard the Bible being taught often enough for everyone in Washington. Furthermore, Sundays were one of our courting days.

Sally warmly accepted Lewis as my "childhood sweetheart;" they had a great rapport. He was a perfect gentleman. Most of the female club members had a beau and clean-up time was our extra time to be with our "main squeezes." Following one of our parties Lewis slowly strolled behind me, embraced me around the waist and whispered in my ear. "I know that I'm not a club member, but may I stay and help with your chores?"
Enthusiastically, I did a half turn, planted a quixotic kiss on his lips and moaned. "Oooh yes!"
Unaware that Sally had witnessed my naughty move, she immediately separated us. Questioning our behavior lead her to ask Lewis his age. I quickly intervened. "He just had a birthday, he turned eighteen." Well, I was half right, he had just celebrated a birthday; he turned twenty-four. Lewis did not correct me. This was the beginning of a two-year off and on relationship before marriage.

Dating was allowed but we had to at least double date, more if possible. There was a way of getting around that barrier. My cousin and I planned our dates where as we would meet at a certain corner at an appointed time. This worked for months, then it came to a horrifying end when I was more than an hour late getting back to our meeting place. Needless to say, she had gone home without me. We were both grounded.

I was an expert at concocting strategies. Sally would never stop anyone from going to the library or joining a study group. I may have lied to get out of the house but I wasn't doing anything inappropriate. Usually I was just five houses down the street at Lewis's cousin house. Her mother was a devout Christian, she would never allow any "hanky panky" in her home. If she had known that I was there without permission, I would have been asked to leave.

Our first summer together Lewis did an internship and studies in North Carolina, at Duke University. The first week was so lonely for me. That's when I realized that I had fallen in love. There was just no way that I could have gone six weeks without seeing Lewis. I'd sit by the phone, hoping that he would call. When he did call we both confessed our desires to see the other . My mental calculator started computing when he mentioned in one of our phone conversations how much he missed me and wished that I was there. His offer to help with the plane fare was all I needed to hear. A friend's mother, unaware of our plot called Sally and invited me over for a weekend. The Wednesday before my weekend stay was due, my friend told her mother that we had family plans and I wouldn't be coming over. Doing this on Wednesday gave our parents time to reconfirm my visit. They didn't. On Friday morning with the help of my "partners in crime" I flew out of town. The thought of sharing two nights with my "honey-honey" made me as happy as a "Sissy in a camp."

BOY!!

OH BOY!

Was I ever wrong.

Lewis was "Holier-Than-Thou." A starched Catholic. I thought, "this man must be afraid of the "moment" or he's a homosexual." That was the most frustrating weekend that I've ever endured. I had put forth such an attentive effort to make my dreams a reality. Not having enough money to purchase a negligee and didn't want to arouse Sally's suspicions by asking for more money, I borrowed one; a red sexy one. That was all for naught; it never came out of my suitcase. My hormones were working overtime, only to be immobilized by a quick hug and kiss upon my arrival, being escorted to the motel where he had reserved my room, sharing another hug and kiss before he left for a class. My visit didn't rate among cutting class. Two evenings were spent on short walks around campus, dinner at some dinky eatery in the company of a couple from his class. Our evenings ended with a good night kiss at my door so he could go study. I cried myself to sleep both nights.

Oh, let me not forget his "special treat". A few hours before I was due to leave, he treated me to an ice cream sundae topped with whip cream and nuts. To add insult to injury, he tried to affectionately spoon feed me. By this time I only wanted to wash his face with his "treat". I told him that I was feeling too sick to eat anything. That was no lie. I was sick of the whole weekend.

Arriving back home, my friends were waiting for me at National Airport. They were all keyed up, demanding details of my "sizzling" week-end. After hearing my story they were bewildered. One asked, "what was on that man's mind?" "Girl, I'd get rid of him," said another one. They exemplified much sympathy and regret for me having such an unsatisfying experience.

Reaching home accompanied by my alibi's left Sally none the wiser. After spending a few minutes with the family I rushed upstairs to my room. There I wrote my first "Dear John" letter.

I did get caught in my lies a few times, but never on my real outlandish adventures. I never told Lewis how I expected to spend my weekend get away. I didn't want to destroy his concept of a "perfect weekend." The break-up didn't last long either. Seeing him again erased all my madness.

Our overall courtship wasn't too unhappy, matter of fact we

had some special highlights. Being an entertainer he liked to attend the shows at the Howard Theater. Some of the artistes would throw things out to the audience. Lewis caught a cuff link from James Brown and presented it to me in a elegant manner. That made me feel peerless.

We shared some embarrassment as well. As sweet as Sally was, she could definitely destroy a young lady's admirable self esteem. Coming home one day finding only Lewis and me in the basement alone, she terminated all home visits without an adult being home. We were downstairs listening to music under red lights. We were merely dancing. Lewis was teaching me the "Bop", one of the dances of our day. He was so smooth on his feet, I just wanted to be an equal dance partner. Yes, the music did have deep sensual meanings. Listening to Smokey, Marvin, the Temptations and all the greats could have easily inspired the love bug to bite under different circumstances but not with the Holy ex alter boy. I wished that Sally could have known the real deal. Instead she made a quizzical confession as she replaced the light bulbs with one hundred watts.

"Believe me Lewis, I'm doing this for your protection. It's Dee that I have to watch. She's as hot as a torpedo, probably ready to explode right now."

Lewis didn't know how to respond to that one. He just gave her an inert smile.

Lewis was a superficial romanticist. Everyone would tell me how much he loved me. He displayed it well in public. Behind close doors he wore a suit of cement. I couldn't penetrate it no matter how hard I tried. There was a lot to be desired in that area but he had a voice and a body that could melt any iceberg. Those attributes and his aspirations of becoming a doctor drew me to him like a magnet. I had no quandary talking about our future together. We discussed marriage many times. However, I had no idea that he meant so soon.

I could have been floored with a feather on Christmas morning of my eleventh grade school year. Lewis came to our door concealing something behind his back. He stepped in our vestibule and ordered me to close my eyes. He placed the open ring box in my hand. As I opened my eyes and saw what I was holding brought on a mixture of feelings. Holding my hands, he proposed. "Dee, I love you, will you please be my wife?"
Indeed, I wanted to be a part of Lewis, I sure didn't want to lose him but this wasn't my dream proposal. I had hoped to receive a dozen of long stemmed roses with a ring attached to one of the stems or positioned in one of the buds. Lewis was suppose to have been on one knee spilling the most inner feelings of his heart as he asked for my hand in marriage. Though, through tears I did say,

"YES!!."

Sally came from the kitchen to check out all the commotion. Searching for words, I just handed her the ring box. To our surprise she gave us her blessings along with a "just in case" warning to Lewis. "Remember, once you're married you're not allowed to bring her back."

Lewis wanted to get married the coming June. Six months away, I was still in high school. I'm sure that Sally thought this was just an engagement for sometime in the future. I didn't have much time clarify her understanding.

The following months became very trying. Everything that could possibly go wrong did. Just finishing the school year was nearly impossible. News of my short engagement unfolded throughout the school. A couple of teachers confronted me and advised me to discuss this with my guidance counselor. I did, but my counselor was not successful in discouraging me. My two best friends were there to console me. However, their mothers tried to terminate our friendships. I could no longer call or visit their homes; for fear that I might "spoil" their daughters. The joke was on them, it was their daughters who were sexually active at that time, not me. Though, this was not by choice. Without their parents blessings or knowledge we managed to survive that storm. Both girls were in my wedding party.

Our major problem was getting a marriage license. I was not yet eighteen and Sally had not legally adopted us. The only option we had was to turn to Daddy who was somewhat estranged. We received financial support through the courts but never a letter or phone call from Daddy. Information concerning him came through Aunt Mabel. She would call or have someone to write us. We would go down to visit during the summer. We also visited grandmother, where we occasionally saw Daddy. Our visits with him were muted therefore they were short.

Lewis felt that he could deal with Daddy. "After all, this will give me an opportunity to get acquainted with my father-in-law," Lewis said.

Lewis and I took the Trailway Bus to Danville, Virginia. I updated him on my family's social skills and what to expect from Aunt Mabel during our ride down. He wasn't too surprised. He was born in Washington but his family had also come from the south, Thomasville, North Carolina.

Uncle Robert and Aunt Mabel met us at the station. They both fell in love with Lewis. Uncle Robert was getting slow, still quiet. Aunt Mabel's behavior had not changed a bit. No one could get a word in during the trip from town. She just had to carry out her one woman act for Lewis; giving him advice on marriage and how to treat me.

"Now if y'u mar' dis gal, y'u bet'a do hu ri't, 'cause she don' tak' no mess. She'll kil' ya sho' as da worl'. She put'n ne'r kil'ed hu dad'y to or three times."

She went over the entire story, telling how she had to rescue us and send us to Washington.

We went directly to grandmother's house from the bus station. That's where Daddy was living. He was home and "thank God" sober. They were expecting us. Grandma had gotten old and hard of hearing; everything had to be repeated several times. After getting all the family's goings-ons and down falls out of the way, Lewis turned to Daddy and made me proud.

"Mr. Lloyd, there's a special cause that have us here today. I'm deeply in love with your daughter. May I have her for my wife? If so, are you willing to sign this consent form?"

Aunt Mabel gave a somber grunt. I spoke within my heart, "Lord please keep her mouth shut." He did. Water was visible in Daddy's eyes but he didn't allow it to flow. He exhibited the same look that I remembered from Mama's death; as though he had lost everything. I was aching to tell him that it didn't have to be that way, we can still be a family. Like all the other times I didn't say a word.

Daddy slowly agreed to sign; proclaiming that he wouldn't do anything to stop my happiness. Both Daddy and grandma was satisfied with my choice for a husband. Grandma asked Lewis to promise her that he would be a good husband to me. Lewis quickly vowed loudly. "Grandma, I will love and cherish her all the days of my life." Lewis's vow didn't have to be repeated for Grandma. She wished us well as I kissed her good-bye and we all left for the little country grocery store up the road; the owner was a notary public.

A heavy-set, tobacco chewing white man met us at the door. After spitting a mouth full of tobacco juice to the side of the store, he invited us in. Yes, Aunt Mabel was the leader. First she reminded Mr. Moore who I was. He slowly admitted that he wouldn't have recognized me, I'd grown so. His store was within walking distant from our house when we lived with Daddy. Beth and I was in his store practically everyday. Bobbing his head toward Lewis, Mr. Moore asked, "who is this boy?" Gosh, did that word "boy" strike a nerve. I wanted to tell him that Lewis was not a boy, probably more man than he, but remembering what we had come for cooled me down. Anyhow, Aunt Mabel had already started her explanation. "Dis is da boy dats gonna mar dis gal. Dat's why we'a hea'e. Da want y'u to fix dare papas."

Lewis pulled the papers from his pocket and handed them to Mr. Moore. Walking over to the counter, Mr. Moore called Daddy over to sign on the appropriate line. He asked Aunt Mabel to witness it. She could sign her name. Again my anger flared when Mr. Moore shook Daddy's hand as he made his "boy" statement. "Look like this boy is gonna be a fine son-in-law." Daddy agreed with a smile. "Yes sir, I believe so."

After getting everything signed and sealed we went back to my uncle's and aunt's house to rest until it was time to go back to Danville.

As we all got out of the car Uncle Robert invited Lewis and Daddy to follow him. "Lis'n, com' he'e boy. Le' me see wha' kinda man y'u is. Lis'n, hope-got-may kil' me, I ain't ly'n, to ya, I got som'n out he'e da'll gro' new ha'r."
Soon we were reliving Aunt Mabel's intrusive demands.
"Now Roe't, don'cha sta't dat drank'n, y'u kno' dat we's gotta geet des chul'en bac' to to'n.
Uncle Robert kept walking toward the corn crib as though nothing was being said. Aunt Mabel and I went in the house where I stretched out across the bed for a nap.

A few hours later I awoke from my nap. I walked outside and found the three passed out under the influence. Daddy was sitting on the ground propped against the crib. Uncle Robert and Lewis had apparently been sitting in the doorway, now they were laying backward in the crib with their feet hanging on the ground. It took a lot of shaking and calling to arouse them. From a water faucet on the side of the house I washed Lewis face and head. He couldn't remember how much or even what he had consumed. After a couple of throw-ups we all left for the bus stations.

Lewis slept the entire trip back to Washington. He stumbled off the bus holding his head with both hands. The most important thing was that we were back in D.C. with our signed and sealed permission slip for marriage.

Beth was working fulltime. She and Sally gave me a budget for the wedding. Our plans were not extravagant. A matron of honor, three bride's maids, three groomsmen, one flower girl, one ring bearer, a train carrier and the best man made up the wedding party. Other than Lewis's limited guest list he made one other request. He wanted "Ave Maria" to be the solo before our union prayer and wanted one of his buddies to sing it. This all seemed simple enough but he hired a coordinator when he saw the perplexing problems that I was having. She was truly God sent.

Disenchantment never eluded us. Three weeks before the wedding I received a "gut-wrenching" phone call from Lewis.
"Dee, I've got to talk with you today."
My heart started pounding rapidly and felt as though it was coming out through my mouth. I was thinking what I would tell my family and friends when Lewis dump me. I didn't ask for any details. I didn't want to be abandoned over the phone. I agreed to

meet him. "At least doing this now is better than being left at the alter," I thought.

I could literally see my clothes shaking on my body as I arrived at his mother's house. Hesitantly I lifted the knocker on the door. Lewis opened the door. He was clutching a letter. As he handed the letter to me I saw the words "Selective Service" on the envelope. I did not bother to read the letter. I only noticed his reporting date.

JUNE 26!

MY BIRTHDAY!

TWO DAYS AFTER OUR WEDDING DAY!

Lewis was hyperventilating as he tried to talk. "I received this a couple of days ago. I didn't know how to tell you. If you choose to put the wedding on hold, I'll understand, but as you see, if we get married now we won't have much time together."

I fell in the nearest chair as the tears flowed like a water fall. "What's next?" My soul asked.

Lewis fell on his knees in front on me; laid his head on my lap and we wept. Momentarily I wished that he had attempted to dump me. I was sure that our love was strong enough to mend whatever the problems would have been. This situation could not be fixed; not even with our strong love. Finally, I laid my head on his and mumbled. "We'll go on with the ceremony."

I didn't tell Sally or Beth that Lewis would be leaving me two days after the wedding. I feared that they would insist that I wait until his service duty was over. I didn't need any more doubts.

Getting through the next couple of weeks was like trying to put a puzzle together and find that some of the pieces are missing. How do you make it come together? Where do you go from here? I knew myself. I knew what and who I wanted and was willing to fight hell's fire to get and keep it. Not once was I apprehensive of the giant step that I was about to take. I was only worried about all of my misfortunes, wondering if they would destroy our marriage.

Lewis was Catholic, I was Baptist, we could not get married in a Catholic Church without me converting to Catholicism and agreeing to raise all children as Catholic. That, I was not willing to do. We agreed to get married in the Baptist Church.

Uncle Paul was against the marriage from the beginning. He had nothing to do with it. Lewis strongly promised that I would finish school and go on to college but his promises fell on deaf ears. Uncle Paul refused to give me away or attend the wedding. I did not invite Daddy for fear of rejection. Uncle Robert and Aunt Mabel was attending the wedding so I requested Uncle Robert's assistance. Because he was not there for any of the rehearsals, my coordinator and I had to work with him on the morning of the wedding. He had gotten to a bottle before we got to him. Basically I was his crutch.

MARRIED! WIFE! All this was ambiguous to me. I was numb. After three rehearsals the aisle appeared ten times longer and bridal jitters kept me crying the entire ceremony. The preparatory prayer performance of Ave Maria really made the service. Being received as a wife by my husband strengthened my willingness to face whatever may befall us.

Our battle started sooner than we anticipated. As we were ready to leave the church the limousines had not arrived. Lewis had ordered two limos; one for us, the matron of honor and the best man, the other one for the rest of the wedding party. When he called the company he was told that the cars were in Northeast Washington looking for us. We were in Northwest waiting for them. After waiting for more than an hour we all took private cars.

Having the reception at Lewis's parents house was the smartest move of all. This was also to be our home until we got our place. Everything was going well. More people attended the reception than at the wedding. We got through all of the traditional hoopla just fine. Beth caught the bouquet. The food was superb. Lewis and I shared the first slice of cake. Our gifts were numerous and germane. Sometime during the evening while toasting and celebrating with our friends the "spirits" overtook us.

The next morning I woke dressed only in my under garments. I had no idea how I got to bed and Lewis was not beside me. The room was spinning too fast for me to steady myself. My clothes had not been unpacked. The party dress that I had worn was left at the foot of the bed. I must have fallen back on the bed at least a half dozen times trying to get the dress. Fortunately our bedroom was next to the bathroom. I crawled in and tried to rid myself of the many toasts that I shared the night before.

Trying to be as quiet as possible so I wouldn't wake Lewis's parents, I set out to find my husband. The stairway was plummeting and rising like a roller coaster. I skidded downstairs on my buttocks. Lewis was asleep on the couch, still in his tuxedo. I pulled a pillow from the couch and fell asleep on the floor beside him. There was no consummation that night or any night for two months.

My mother-in-law had less than a day to get Lewis sober and off to Ft. Bragg. I was too sick to help or see him off. My birthday nearly slipped by. Lewis had already gotten my present. As he was about to leave he came in our bedroom and gave me a gold charm bracelet with one charm, a bride; my first birthday as his wife. As precious as his gift was, I could not lift my head off the pillow. His kiss on my forehead was our good-byes.

Lewis wasn't altogether himself, but he had drank before

and could handle it better than me. He took the Greyhound to Ft. Bragg, North Carolina. That was approximately a nine hour ride, I'm sure that he slept the majority of those hours. It was two days before he called me.

CHAPTER SIX

Living with my in-laws required a great deal of adjusting. A huge three story four bedroom row house was spacious enough. My father-in-law was a World War I Veteran, thirty years older than his wife. He spent his days doing chores around the house. We were never close but we respected each other and I addressed him as dad. My mother-in-law was a supervisor of housekeeping in a hospital in Virginia. She left for work early because she used public transportation and was due there by seven. We were close. I had no problem calling her mom. Their youngest child was a junior high student, he recognized me as a big sister.

My first week was spent in seclusion nursing my hangover demons. I came out of my room only when necessary. My mother-in-law checked on me often, giving me crackers, ginger ale and aspirin for the headaches.

Ma Martha's words kept ringing in my heart, "strong drinks

are the work of the devil." Believe me, the devil was doing a job on me. I wondered how anyone could drink something that would make them feel like this? I promised myself, "if I ever get over this stomach-churning, head spinning sickness I will never touch an alcoholic beverage again."

I started missing Lewis and wondering how I would spend the next eight weeks. To keep myself somewhat occupied, I'd walked to the library some days to study. This would keep me abreast of the school work that I would be taking soon. I wrote Lewis at least three time a week. He called whenever he could. Our conversations always boosted my morale.

At last, the end of August arrived. Lewis came home for fifteen days. We celebrated his birthday which was the fourth of August. That wasn't the only essence of our celebration. Each passing day was more captivating than the day before. I wish that I could claim rights to the saying, "anything worth having is worth waiting for." I also would like to make it known to the originator that I should be honored for holding the waiting record.

Married life proved to be a little promising. I enrolled in night school. Lewis went with me a few nights. He carried my books as we strolled down the halls hand in hand. I explained to my instructors that he was home only for a few days and we would like to spend this time together. Only one teacher asked him to wait outside the classroom.

Lewis performed with his group on his last weekend home. As he was about to lead a song he stopped and offered a few words. First he thanked the group for including him in the performance, then he introduced me to the audience in an affectionate mode. It was enthralling to hear him say these words. "I'm dedicating this song to a very special lady, the love of my life. My darling wife."

I stood and blew him a kiss.

That was an extremely special night. We did something that we'd never done before. After his gig we doubled dated with the guitar player and his sweetheart. The guys had it all planned. Lewis knew that I was a lover of water. In the early morning hour, we ended up at the water front. Haines Point was the spot where lovers went to neck and lay under the stars. I had heard about this place from my friends and wondered why Lewis hadn't acquainted me with this favored site. Claiming a space to spread our blanket was next to impossible. Couples were entangled all around as if they were bedded down for the night. I felt a little guilty about being out with a single couple but they had gone off in a different direction. Lewis and I took a seat on the edge of the grass over looking the Potomac River, facing the Virginia side. We had a perfect view of the lights from the airport. A slight sloshing sound of the water against the sides of the river was so tranquilizing. I rested in Lewis's arms as he continued to soothe me with song. This night I saw another side of Lewis; a passionate, gentle side that I'd always envisioned. I could feel our minds and bodies mutually melting, becoming one. The rising of the sun was our cue to leave.

Time had come for Lewis to leave for Ft. Polk, Louisiana. We did not own a car. Sally came over to drive us to the airport. The thought of being alone again was painful. His training would be more effortful this time. He warned me that he might not be able to call as often as he had before. Sadness filled the atmosphere but I refused to let him become disheartened. Sally and I kept laughter aboard our trip to the airport.

Studying and writing Lewis kept my days worry free. It wasn't until I started having morning sickness a month or so after Lewis left that I nearly exploded with joy. When the doctor confirmed my pregnancy I was indeed overwhelmed. In addition, hearing that the due date was in June thrilled me even more. "An anniversary baby". I could hardly wait to get home and call Lewis with the good news. His ebullience could be felt through the phone. We shared profound joy and immediately started planning our baby's future. **"Our baby girl's future."** We promised each other with assurance.

The holidays were rapidly coming upon us and Lewis knew

that he wasn't going to be able to come home. We mutually agreed that I would spend Thanksgiving with my family and Christmas I would visit him in Louisiana.

The weeks seemingly flashed by. Just thinking of the seed growing inside of me kept my spirit high. I flew to Louisiana where we spent our first Christmas together. It was sheer happiness for us.

Lewis would leave out early for his duty but he returned early; this gave us the evenings to ourselves. He gave me another charm for my bracelet, a wrapped gift box. I gave him an electric shaver. Our first Christmas as Mr. & Mrs. was a merry one. We started going through names and making educational plans for the baby. As much as we both wished for a girl, we declared that whether it's a boy or girl, our love will not come up short.

Only a couple of weeks into the New Year I was hit with a dose of reality. Happiness and joy for me only meant that misery was on its way. I had come to the realization that I was born just to be tormented. This was my ultimate conclusion when my doctor told me of my health problems. I had developed gestational diabetes and hypertension which could cause serious problems, even loss of the baby. Because of the many spontaneous miscarriage threats I was hospitalized days, sometimes weeks at the time. I got up-set with the doctors and their continuous reminders of my condition. I felt that they were waiting for me to miscarry.

During one of my hospital stays I almost agreed with the doctor to terminate the pregnancy. Just thinking of the jubilation that Lewis expressed over the holidays made me want to fight that much harder for our baby. When asked the last time about termination, I adamantly responded. "Hell no. I'm only willing to lose my life trying to save my baby." Seeing my frustrations my doctor offered a little speculative hope. "Now we can't promise you anything, your life as well as the baby's is in danger at this moment but if you can make it to the seventh month your chances could be favorable." He continued, saying that they may be able to induce labor or perform a cesarean section at that time. I agreed to try his proposal, stating, "if you see where one must go, to save the other, please save my baby."

Doctor's orders were taken seriously. I did everything that I was told to do. I had to drop out of school and for the next four months I practically lived in the hospital.

I didn't want to burden Lewis with the situation at home. Yet, I could not hide it for long. While I was hospitalized he would call home and his mother kept telling him that I wasn't home, as I had asked her to do. Jealousy crept into Lewis's mind. He accused me of having an affair or running around with my old school buddies. That infuriated me. How could he even entertain the thought of me frolicking around while carrying his child? My immature actions weren't any better. I called his barracks and left a frightening message with one of his comrades. I asked him to tell Lewis that I was in the hospital and the baby and I was dying. A message that I wanted to retract as soon as I hung up the phone. Thinking that I had spoken into existence a demising end for our baby worried me more than how Lewis may feel or respond.

With the help of his mother and through the American Red Cross, Lewis was able to verify my condition and locate me. The next evening he entered my hospital room. We held each other, wept and asked each other for forgiveness, promising never to withhold anything from each other again.

Unless the doctors had deemed it essential for Lewis to stay, he had to leave in two days. We didn't request more time on his visit. All reports were hopeful. We were told that the baby was developing well with no apparent abnormalities. I was allowed to spend one night at home. Lewis monitored my every breath. He walked me to the bathroom, even bathed me. He didn't want me to use any extra energy. Everything was placed at my finger tips. This was to be my yo-yo routine but we were determined to work with it.

The following day Lewis got me back to the hospital around

midday. He left for his trip back to the base. I assured him that he needn't worry. I was well cared for. Sally and Beth visited almost every day and his mother came when she could. Friends were in and out as well. I really didn't care for too many visitors. Other than all the IV's, medications and complete bed rest my hospital stay wasn't bad.

At last, the day of reckoning had come. On the morning of April 3 1968, I was given several injections and was taken to the delivery room. I can't recall what all took place but a great deal of time had passed when I was awakened in a recovery room with six or more new mothers. A nurse was making rounds calling out to each one, name by name, stating the weight and sex of her child. After about the fourth name and another boy, I thought that I was in the "boys" recovery room. I quickly reminded myself of my promised words. "Whether a boy or girl I will be thankful". When the nurse reached me and made sure that I was awake and responsive, she announced the birth of a girl but no weight. Nevertheless, from that moment on, I felt no pain. I was ready to shower and go to my little girl.

"Not now." I was told. "Your baby is resting in an incubator, you won't be able to hold her just yet."

My gallantry was dampened. I knew of all the risks that we were taking. I had to converse with myself to continue to fight. I kept repeating, "everything is alright now, the baby is here and I am still alive."

As I was being situated to be rolled out to a room on the ward, I was told that my husband was there and had been there all night. "All night?" I asked myself. That mean that I'd been there over twenty-four hours. I must have really been knocked out. I didn't remember a thing. My temper began to rise. I had not been told anything about the procedures that had been done or the condition of the baby.

It was pacifying to see Lewis entering my room. He was bearing a dozen of roses for me and a single rose for the baby.

Immediately I sensed something was wrong with Lewis. Oh, he was happy about the baby. He gave me the whole story of her birth, how I had delivered her without the C-section. He had been watching her for hours through the nursery window. Laughing, he commented that she was going to be in gymnastics because she is kicking already. Yet, a suspicious look veiled his face and he couldn't hide it.

Authorities in Washington were grappling, trying to regain control in the city. Dr. Martin Luther King Jr. had been assassinated and chaos was throughout the city. Many disloyal protestors took an avenue that Dr. King would have never approved. They burned and looted businesses as though that would resurrect Dr. King. The National Guard had to be called in to help restore peace. Maneuvering around town was complicated for the working people. A curfew had been initiated; one could be arrested if caught in the streets without meeting the city's guidelines. Lewis had no problem going or coming because he was in uniform. Family and friends couldn't visit for weeks.

My chances for watching our little angel were limited but I tried to be at the nursery window when the nurses were caring for her. She was so tiny. The thought of changing her name to Angel or Miracle crossed my mind but we had settled on Devonne. Lewis brought her a rose everyday, even though we couldn't place them in the nursery. We kept them in my room to remind us of our blessing.

I remained in the hospital two weeks after giving birth. This, I didn't mind; I was close to my baby. My health woes were somewhat under controlled. I was no longer being treated for diabetes. The blood pressure was more severe. The stress and worry kept it up, I'm sure.

Amid all of our happiness Lewis's countenance was undeniable weighty. I knew that there was something that he wasn't sharing with me. When I firmly approached him, his eyes became teary as he made known the dreadful news.

"Dee, I have orders to Viet Nam."

A ton of bricks couldn't have been any heavier on my heart. I was already lying down. A gargantuan death desire swept through me. "If I could only close my eyes and die." Using my last bit of stamina I sat up on my bed, took Lewis's hands and secured them in mine and jump started his faith. "Honey, don't you dare start worrying or doubting our faith now. There's nothing that can bring us down. Our love is strong enough to fight any battle; even Viet Nam." He held me close and we cried together. Finally he spoke from a "soldiers heart."

"Dee I love you. I love my country, but I hate this thing called WAR. Do you realize that there is a possibility that we may never see each other again? Our daughter may never know me or know how much I love her." I closed his lips with one finger.

"Don't you talk like that. We've just overcome the largest possible obstacle. Just four months ago the doctors wanted to terminate our pregnancy but our faith prevailed. We can't give up now."

While I was still talking Lewis started writing in the baby's album. I assumed he was recording the baby's birth. When I looked over his shoulders, I saw that he was writing a letter to God. I named his prayer to God "My Soldier's Prayer."

"Dear God,

> Maker and protector of all mankind, creator of heaven and earth. Keep this my family, walk with them through all their

days, show them that even though I am away from them that I still love them as much now as I did when I was there.

Bless my little wife, keep her from harm and talk to her when she is tempted to go astray. Manifest your divine grace and glory in her everyday life, bless her going out and her coming in, let your wondrous light shine upon her pathways, bless our little daughter, teach her to live the way you would have her, be with her all her days, enrich her life with your powerful love. Bless her accomplishments, company her in her troubles. Be with me on the field of battle, guide my eyes and ears, walk beside me on each mission, give me courage and piece of mind. I ask this of you now and forever, and when I have done this, see me safely home. I ask this in the name of the father, son and Holy ghost."

He didn't stop there, he turned the page. He decided to write a letter to our daughter.

"My Dearest Daughter,
    In the event that I'm sent over seas and some harm should come to me, rest peacefully in the thought that daddy love and wanted to be with you always. But like all men daddy had to go away and fight to make this world a safe place for you to live and learn. Take care of your mother and be a good girl. Always reach out for the finer things in life and live on the Godly side. And now my lovely daughter daddy will close this note but never his heart or love for you. My heart is filled with sorrow at this time because I'm leaving you, but if it be God's wish I'll be back soon.
    Sincerely yours,
    Daddy"

When he finished writing, I took the book, held it close to my heart and softly agreed. "Amen."

Lewis did accomplish a few things during his stay. He found us an apartment in upper Northwest on Euclid Street, near Meridian Park. Living in our own place was perfect. It wasn't fully decorated but we had all of the necessities. Our wedding gifts certainly improved the appearance of our kitchen, bathroom and bedroom. Likewise with baby gifts. We barely had to purchase anything. Beth moved in with us. She stocked baby clothes galore; from newborn to twenty-four months. The newborn was too large for Devonne but we made do. "Hazel" became Beth's name around the house; symbolizing her housekeeping and cooking capabilities.

It was extremely stressful for me to go home, leaving our baby behind. She was progressing faster than the doctors had expected. We were allowed to hold her for short periods at a time. I couldn't hold her alone, she was too small. Usually a nurse or Lewis would hold her on my lap, even then I was panicky. We spent our days at the hospital with her.

The doctors knew that Lewis would be leaving in a few days so they allowed us to bring Devonne home. They saw no serious problems and she had already been upgraded to the regular nursery. This should have been the happiest day in any parent's life. I was indeed overjoyed to have our baby home. Yet, I was as equally sad in the same moment. This also meant that time was running out for Lewis. His orders to Viet Nam had to be filled.

Because of Devonne's size we were afraid to put her in the crib. We kept her in our bed. Lewis's emotions would get the best of him when he attempted to change or feed her. He was fearful that his parenting years would not come to pass. Neither of us knew what to say to the other. There was complete silence for long periods at a time. Then there were times when we just held each other without uttering a word.

I may have been lost for words in the natural but I remembered all those spirit filled prayers of old. Our last night together was spent lying in Lewis's arms praying and crying out to the Lord in the spirit.

The following day was like preparing for a funeral. I was moving out of instincts. Nothing seemed to have a meaningful motive. Lewis purposely distant himself. He had a four o'clock reservation out of National Airport to Oakland, California where he would make connections to Viet Nam. Beth was there to keep Devonne while Sally and I took him to the airport. Around two-thirty Lewis gave the baby one last kiss as the tears rolled. He reached for me and embraced the both of us as we shared our frantic emotions. We despairingly left for the airport.

We reached the airport with time to spare. I couldn't hold it any longer. I just boohooed. We comforted each other in the car before going inside. I stayed with him and shared our last kiss before he boarded the plane. He promised to call me from Oakland.

I had to press on through the weeks ahead. Beth was there for the baby and me after work. Caring for Devonne kept me busy during the day. Now weighing a little more than five pounds she was still too fragile for me to be comfortable handling. I made a pallet on the floor for her. I even bathed her there for fear of dropping her. If it wasn't for supporting her little head, you could hold her in your hand as a ball. On her doctor's appointment days Beth would take a few hours off to help me. Overall she was a good baby. She slept most of the night and when she did wake up all I had to do was dry her and give her a little formula and she'd sleep for hours again. This left a lot of night time for me to worry and cry. I watched all the news on television and read the two local newspapers. Every fatality sent chills over me. There appeared to be fatalities everyday.

The hardest task was waiting for Lewis's letters to start coming. It took about three weeks for me to get the first letter. I had several letters and pictures ready to mail. I wrote frequently and sent care packages, enough for him to share. Every letter that he sent I'd read them to Devonne, hoping that she could feel her daddy's love. I could sense from his letters that the conditions there were contemptible. He shared a lot of concern for his safety. His job was assisting the wounded and getting them back to medical facilities, as well as retrieving the deceased. He told me about a few horrifying situations. Through it all his faith didn't waver, he ended most of his letters with a prayer.

With the help of Sally and Beth I got back in night school and finished. Mental normality was finding its way back in our lives. Lewis called several times on the "short-waved radio". We contained our emotions during our verbal communications. I shared a great deal of Devonne's progress, even allowed her to "ga-ga" over the radio. My packages to him were well received, some of his buddies sent thanks.

The months were rolling by, though not as fast as we wished. I started getting a little restless being home. I found a job in a local hospital as a nurse's aid. This was an excellent move. Lewis and I had planned on being a "doctor/doctor," or "doctor/nurse couple." This hospital had a nursing school and I would work my way through. Lewis wasn't too pleased about me working but knowing who I had to baby sit eased his concerns. Besides we could use the funds. A wife's allotment wasn't that much. Lewis had his pay check sent home and Beth took on a share of the bills. My little income allowed us to add to our savings account.

Countdown was in full swing. Everyday I marked a day off the calander and noted the number of days left. In Lewis's letters he started mentioning "short time", meaning that it won't be long before he'll be home. In his letters he also mentioned that he was thinking of making a career of the army. He felt that making a career was a sure way of finishing his education and providing us with the life style that we had talked about. I really didn't think much of his idea but I wanted to support him in any of his undertakings. through love I teased him saying, "you are the rooster of this coop, wherever you lead, the hen and chicks will follow."

Beth and I started planning a big celebration for Lewis's return home. She purchased the ingredients for all of his favorite dishes. Devonne had her communication skills in tack, she could say "da-dy, stop now, no, lets eat, I'm sor-ry, I won't do, and many more cute sayings. I cleaned and rearranged our bedroom. This much happiness alone should have frightened me.

Sure enough, with just weeks to go I took Devonne for a walk one morning. Upon reentering our building I spotted two army officers searching the tenant's list. Noticing that one officer had his finger under my name I started crying and I asked the obvious.

"He's dead, isn't he?"

They looked at each other and requested my name. After identifying myself they introduced themselves and offered to escort me to my apartment. With their help I opened my mailbox. There laid a letter from Lewis. My legs nearly buckled under me. One officer took Devonne, the other one supported me. We took the elevator to my floor. Entering my apartment and with much sympathy the officers explained that Lewis was a victim of an explosion. His vehicle had rolled over a mine while he was out getting the wounded. He suffered the loss of his limbs but lived several hours and was flown to a hospital, where he died from his injuries. At this point I was hysterical. With their help I made an attempt to called Beth at work. I wasn't able to talk. An officer took the phone and told Beth the news. I heard him tell her that they would stay with me until a family member could get there. Very little else can I remember.

Days out of my life were lost. I felt that I was locked in a bad dream and could not break loose.

The army did an excellent job in getting his remains home via Dover Air Force Base. They also assisted with all the arrangements. We had a local mortician to receive the remains in Delaware.

My mother in-law asked if we could have the wake at her

house. I had not seen that since I left North Carolina and wasn't sure if it could be done. The original Funeral Director would not accommodate us, but after calling around, we found one that would. The flag covered coffin sat in my mother in-law's front room overnight with a soldier standing at each end, changing every hour or so.

I'd received several letters from Lewis after the day of the dreadful news. Yet, on the morning of his funeral I chose to open the one that came on the day that the news came. He seemed so happy that his time in Viet Nam wasn't long. Getting back to us was all that mattered to him. He stated that "nothing, not even death could keep us apart now." I read those words over and over again, hoping that somehow a mistake had been made. After all the casket was sealed, maybe the names had gotten mixed somehow, not that I was wishing this much pain on someone else. I kept telling myself that any moment the phone will ring, someone would be asking us to stop the funeral, or an officer will come to the door to make the correction. That call never came, an officer did not appear.

Lewis's funeral was held at the same Catholic Church that refused to marry us. The church services, including me entering the church escaped me. I only recall the twenty-one-gun salute at the gravesite, for every shot pierced my already emaciated heart.

No, Lewis is no longer here in person but his spirit will live forever. His remains are resting in Arlington National Cemetery, along with a part of me.

PART TWO: VICTORY IS MINE

CHAPTER SEVEN

Death does not necessarily mean that one is dead. I was alive yet dead to my surroundings. I only wished that I was buried. Caring for Devonne or myself was nearly impossible. Thoughts of ending it all were strongly wrestling with my spirit. I was continually being shown evil methods of becoming a family on the other side. I was sure to take Devonne with me. I wouldn't leave her behind to be tossed around as I had been. My nights were filled with dreams, even nightmares. I. E. and Ma Martha was always praying. Lewis would hold me and we would pray and cry together. Never was there any advice from anyone. I suppose I was expecting Lewis to ask me to come to him. All this torture would finally wake me. My pillow would be drenched with tears. Life became so depressing and miserable. I was in an anesthetized state. I quit my job, stopped answering my door or telephone.

Sally and Uncle Paul was forced to gain entry by the way of the resident manager when they got no response from me after trying for hours. I was sitting on the couch with Devonne on my lap as they walked through the door. I lied, pretending to either have been asleep or out during their calls. I didn't know how to tell them that I was contemplating suicide.

After months of moping, crying, and deteriorating, I realized that my state of mind was not healthy for me or the baby. I had to make a desperate attempt to start over.

The changes in my life style had become so peculiar it frightened me. I was looking for perfection in everyone. Friends would sat up blind dates and introduce me to their circle of friends. Nothing satisfied me. I had out grown all those school days insecurities. I was searching for Lewis's qualities. A real man, certainly not the jolly seeking, over aged boys who was pawning themselves off as men.

My mother in-law offered her recuperating advice willingly. "Honey, if you want to be happy, find yourself an old man. An old man will make you his queen."
That shouldn't have been a problem for me. I'd always been attracted to older sophisticated gentlemen.

What friends I had left dissociated themselves when I started degrading their opinions and choices of companions. None were or had been married, though two did have a child each. I felt that they were settling for much less than they should.

As time moved on and a few failed relationships I took a good look at myself. I had to judge my worth. I learned that I could go to college through the G.I. Bill. First I decided to sharpen my math and writing skills through a free adult education program before enrolling in a university. I also worked parttime as a nurse's aid through various health care agencies. Working through an agency allowed me to work around my schedule. My widow's pension, salary and school money allowed me to put Devonne in a private nursery school. She enjoyed her school and all of her little friends. This kept me efficient for a while but the dreams started repeating themselves. I was being haunted so frequently I was forcing myself to stay awake at night. I knew that I had to fight to maintain stability for my child's sake.

Beth had gotten her own place but she kept Devonne sometime, giving me a break. She had met Larue, a long distant truck driver. He was also from North Carolina, just a few miles from our hometown. They knew a lot of the same people, went to the same school. Larue, being a few years older, disallowed their acquaintance while in North Carolina. They started making their nuptials plans. After all Beth did catch my bouquet. This would have been my first wedding ceremony since my own. I couldn't go through with it as much as I wanted to be there. She had a house wedding. It was simple but gorgeous. Sally and Uncle Paul had a walkway with an arch leading around the house. Grapes were grown around the arch. The grapevines were arranged to give the appearance that the bride and groom were standing in the midst of the vines. The reception was held in the back yard. Pictures were my only view. I took a trip out of town.

Like me, Beth started her family right away. Less than a year she gave birth to a nine pound boy. Two years later a seven pound girl. The perfect family with so much happiness. She kept her head above the clouds. Washing diapers, cooking and cleaning was her life's dream. I sincerely wished her the very best but my pain was too deep for me to join in her euphoria.

Devonne began to notice the family structure of her friends and questioned me as to why she had no father. This took all of my strength to explain that her father was with her in spirit. She'd draw "stick families" as most children do. Her father was represented by a dot. Sadly, she'd ask me to write spirit for her. Her acceptance of the "spirit dad" was passed on to her dolls. She'd tell them, "your father is here, you just can't see him." That was my explanation to her.

My morale started sinking again. Though I was passing, my studies were suffering. Contentment was out of my reach. I was searching for "something," not sure what. I met some poker players in the neighborhood and started playing cards every weekend. About this same time I started dating a guy from school. He was not an "attention holder," but okay for dining or something to do. He didn't play cards and would get upset when I stood him up to go to a poker game. Needless to say, he didn't hang around long. A few months after our last conversation I received a wedding invitation addressed to me "and card buddies." That was the first wedding that I attended after mine. The poker crew refused to go. I only went because of his sarcastic attitude. A mutual friend of Lewis and mine escorted me. It was a large church wedding. I did shed a tear or two but not because of the loss of him. I was visualizing Lewis and me standing at the alter pledging our love for each other. I went back to the card game that night as though he was just a passing whim.

Gambling wasn't a long term fix either. My social stimulant lost its glamour the night that I was sitting next to a cheater. I had no idea that I was playing with a professional card shark, however, I did notice that this particular guy was winning most of the hands. It wasn't until another player had lost all and left, saying that he will be right back. Everyone thought that he was going for more money. When he returned he pulled a shotgun on the cheater. When the trickster raised his arms, cards fell from his sleeves. All aces and duces. My life flashed before my water filled eyes as I looked down the gun barrel. The gunman made known what he had seen all night and requested only what he had lost. The shark gave up the money and everyone left. This taught me to seek companionship in safer places.

Devonne was as observant as I was at her age. I was going through stages of depression and had problems staying focused but I tried to keep my daily grief from her. Weekday mornings especially, I tried to keep them full of joy as we got ready for school. Breakfast time was always shared. She would place love notes by my plate. They were so loving and encouraging, until one morning I was thunderstruck with a very troubling note.

"Mommy, I know you are not happy. I heard you crying last night. Maybe if I run away, you can be happy".

We both stayed home that day and when we finished hugging and crying we had a long talk. I'm not sure of my exact words but I made it clear to her that she was my happiness. She was all that I had. We kept the hugs, kisses and notes as a part of our daily lives. I didn't want her to experience the loveless state of mind that I had endured. She was still tiny in size but housed such an exceptional mind.

The dreams and visions amplified themselves. Having someone from the grave directing my mere existence in an indirect way seemed worst than the depressive state. I decided to seek help. Not knowing how or where to start, I sought help from a professor as well as doing some research on my own. One thing I did find out was psychologist help was more the "IN" thing than I suspected.

One of my main concerns was the response of my family. Would they be supportive if they knew that I was seeing a therapist, or would they think that I'm a nut? The thought of going out of town seemed appropriate. Gender was another worry. A female would be more susceptible to my problems, I presumed.

I decided not to go out of town. I gathered all the information, listed possible contacts, then cringed as I blindly pulled one from the bunch.

That's one appointment I wished that I'd never made. Knots formed in the pit of my stomach as I walked in a luxurious office of soft blues and mauves. A large painting of calm waters and downy clouds hung behind the receptionist desk. For a moment I was mesmerized; my eyes were fixed on that painting. A lady gently stroked my hand to gain my attention. She was very polite; looked to be in her late thirties to early forties. After getting my information she led me to another office. To my surprise all the myths and expectations vanished. This office was decorated as lavishly as the outer office. There was no couch. Instead comfortable thick cushioned, mauve colored leather arm chairs and a cherry wood semi circle desk decked out the room. Even more surprising the lady whom I thought was the receptionist was the psychologist. Her accomplishments were many. The degrees, certificates and accolades were displayed over the walls. The ice was broken when she introduced herself and family photos which adorned her desk.

It wasn't easy for me to disclose my dreams and the more I tried the more she attempted to convince me that they were my past that I refused to let go. She kept referring back to my childhood. "You can't heal the end without healing the beginning," she stated. Reliving my childhood was not a problem. I didn't need to pay someone to tell me that I was seeking attention when I did my mischievous acts as a child. But to be told now that I am holding on to everyone of the pass and still seeking attention is ludicrous. I agreed with everything else that she said just to utilize the time. I'd decided that I wouldn't be coming back.

I refused to be defeated. I knew that my answers were out there somewhere and it was up to me to find them.

Devonne and I had standing weekend visits over Sally's and Uncle Paul's. Actually that was Devonne's second home. Devonne was their first grandchild and they spoiled her royally. Uncle Paul gave her the run of the house. I was deeply burdened on this

Saturday but we kept our weekly visit. I wasn't optimistic about sharing my problems with Sally. She would probably think that I'm just being ridiculous and start joking about them.

Uncle Paul was home finishing up his weekend cooking as he always did. Every Saturday morning he'd get up as if he was going to work and go over to Fifth Street Farmers Market. "You have to get to the market early, if you want the best foods," was Paul's law. He kept cases of choice cut steaks in the freezer. I believe he ate a steak everyday. Rare, practically raw satisfied his appetite. His roast had to be a certain cut.

Mountain Oysters was another recurrent dish. It was sometime before we knew what we were eating but finding out didn't change our liking for them. He'd smother them with gravy and onions; they tasted like country style steak. His greens or beans had to be crisp and fresh. I had a keen eye for fresh vegetables as well. I'd remembered that from my peddling days. Uncle Paul was a cook in the army and swore that he could cook better than any woman. Growing up we didn't argue with him nor did we challenge him because none of us wanted that job. Keeping the house to his satisfaction was hard enough.

"Come on in here and fix you and the baby a plate," he offered as we walked in. As usual the meal was great. As we were eating a former schoolmate and neighbor stopped by. I had not seen her for a long. Like old times, she fixed herself a plate and joined us at the table. She immediately commented of my facial expression. "Girl, what's wrong with you? You look like you're angry or in pain."

"Both," I replied.

When we finished eating we went out on the front porch and talked. I explained how the dreams were taking over my life. Maryland was amazed as I continued.

"It's like they're dictating the do's and don'ts in my life, yet, they never say a word. They'll just come into view, pray and hug me. Maryland cut in saying, "that's God talking to you."

"God," I asked.

All my life I was taught to have faith in God. But it's because of God that I'm in this situation.

"How can anyone have faith in someone or something that's suppose to be able to fix anything, yet, nothing has been fixed for me?" I asked and continued.

"Look at me. A broken home as a child .

Now, no husband, or a father for my baby. I'm so unhappy I want to die. Now you're telling me that God wants to talk to me? What else can He possibly say or do?"

Maryland promised that she and her mother would help me find the answers. She invited me to a prayer meeting the coming

Tuesday night. Initially I said yes to get her off my back. As Tuesday night approached, I decided to go. Besides what did I have to lose? I was as low as I could possibly go. Up was the only way for me.

That Tuesday night I was raise from the dead. My outlook on life had a purpose. Going to bed and falling asleep was no longer despised. No matter how my dreams began, somehow my love ones were incorporated. Though somehow they were all different now. Mama would appear and smile as bright as the sun. I. E. and Ma Martha would be praising the Lord as they did around our table at meal times. Lewis expressed his approval with spiritual romance.

On one of our affaire de coeur Lewis made a pledge. The only verbal communication in all of his appearances.
"I'm not here with you but happiness will find you, I promise."
He kissed me good-bye before vanishing.
What a puzzling statement; it troubled my mind for a while.

Devonne and I started attending church regularly. We were baptized in the Pentecostal Church of God In Christ Denomination. She joined the youth choir as well being one of the church's soloist. My spiritual growth inspired the pastor to elevate me to youth leader and later junior church mother. Having a desire to do more, Devonne and I initiated a project of our own. Every Thanksgiving and Christmas we gave out boxes of food to the needy. Not that we could afford it; we found joy in sacrificing throughout the year. Before I was licened to drive we delivered the boxes by taxi.

The saying, "no good deed goes unpunished" was proven to be true while we were out spreading Christmas cheer. As we were delivering our first box the taxi driver drove away, stealing the others. Devonne looked at me bewildered with her big bright "daddy's eyes." Before I knew it Ma Martha's spirit was working through me.

"It's alright sweetheart. There are some mean people in the world, but God knows the intent of our hearts and He will deal with that man." This did not discourage us, our missionary work expanded, reaching out to the homeless and the sick. I felt that when I was in my "valley days", God knows they were many, I could have been driven into any abyss. A beacon was always before me, leading me to safety. I compared myself to the Apostle Paul in his writings, especially, 1 Corinthians 15: 10.

"But by the grace of God I am what I am: and His grace which was bestowed upon me was not in vain….."

I must throw out a life line for some deserving soul. If by chance I can reach just one, it'll be well worth the effort.

My salvation came under scrutiny when Rev. Earl came to Washington. He was conducting a revival. I was happy to see him.

I had not seen him since I'd become a widow. He'd aged a bit but still had that distinguished air about him. Because of his great preaching ability he stayed booked throughout the country. Uncle Paul never moved his membership from North Carolina so Rev. Earl was still his pastor and visited whenever he came to town. His conversation clearly verified the scripture of " ravening wolves in sheep's clothing." St. Matthew 7:15 KJV

First he damned my denomination. "You're too young to be in a Holy church. I know their teachings, and they teach against fornication. You'll lose your mind if you don't get a man."

His words sent chills through my body. How could he have deceived so many people? He didn't stop there, with Sally and Uncle Paul sitting there he invited me out for the evening. My reply was sharp, but truthful. "You demon, from the pit of hell. What would the Saunders's say if they could hear you now? You're going to hell for your evil doings."

No remorse or shame was shown. Instead he boasted about his five churches in North Carolina and how they love to give him money. He did tell us that the Saunders were great givers, both to the church and to him.

"They gave me one hundred dollars every month, like clock work." I angrily commented.

"What a waste."

Again, I reminded him that hell will be his final resting place without a change.

I was so busy with my church work, Devonne's school and my student teaching job, I had not given another thought to Lewis's promise. However, as we left church one Sunday I drove out Kennedy Street, a route which was not the norm for me. Standing by a Ford Station Wagon stood a man who looked exactly like Lewis. I panicked but didn't say a word. I jotted the tag number down in the front of my Bible. I was restless until morning.

Monday morning I was standing at the doors of the Motor Vehicle Administration when they opened. I sure hope the Lord has forgiven me for that lie. I told the lady at the window that I had an accident with this gentleman and didn't get all of his information. She gave me his insurance company's name and his phone number.

Now, with information in hand, my mind was bombarded with every possible "what ifs". "What if he's married? What if the car wasn't his? What if he rejects me?" The list grew by the seconds.

Late Monday evening, as nervous as a captured kitten, I made the call. As I was dialing the number, I decided not to use my real name. A man answered on the second ring. His "hello" could have been a recording of Lewis; a deep arousing voice. I'm not sure what my conversation was but I introduced myself as Susan. I must have said something intriguing, he agreed to meet me the next evening after church.

I met Gene Tuesday February 17, 1976. I'd told him that I only wanted him to meet my family and in-laws. However, after meeting him I knew that there would be more. He agreed to meet the family that Friday evening. One terrified phone call produced a twenty plus year relationship.

Introducing Gene was both entertaining and sad. He was well received. Sally, being herself, shouted. "My God! Where did you come from? I thought we'd buried you."
Gene, removing the one thing unlike Lewis, a pipe from his lips as he smiled and responded. "I can assure you, I am not the one you buried."
My mother in-law couldn't contain herself, nearly choked on a "dry swallow."
"Oh my Lord! You're just like Lewis."
Instantly they connected. He started running errands and transporting her to and from our house. She referred to him as her son. Devonne, through her shyness managed to converse as she showed subtle signs of approval.

My real identity was revealed during our family gathering. Gene had a confession to make as well. He thought that I was

Susan's mother the first night we met. I'd just left prayer meeting; was dressed beyond my years, wearning a long skirt and a "Holy hair do" which he thought was a wig on crooked. We all got a wholesome laugh from his story.

Right away we started sharing our lives; seeing each other everyday. Gene was self-employed, his time wasn't too demanding. Many days he'd arrive early enough to have breakfast with us and help get Devonne off to school. He attended Devonne's school events. Dinners were planned to include Gene. We'd become a family.

Our differences in religious beliefs caused quite a bit of discussion but he never condemned my beliefs. He was not affiliated with any church though he was reared in the Presbyterian Faith. As a youth he participated in Bible studies and summer activities. Recognition of a Higher Power had been instilled in him.

Unaware of my habits and certainly not to irritate Gene I found myself sitting at my kitchen table crying and praying after receiving a call from him. He was expected for dinner. His call was to voice his complaint. "Dee, I'm on my way. I have something to say, I'm not sure how to say this."
"What is it?" I asked.
"Dee I love you. I want to be with you. But I can't stand all that humming and praying. You sound like Aunt Jemima, or some

slave woman."

I was crushed.

We had our times when we had to persevere through my private prayer meetings but he learned to accept them.

My peak of happiness was reached the evening when we decided to relax after dinner in front to the television. Devonne had gone to her room to play. Sometime later she tipped in the front room and sat on the couch between Gene and me, closer to Gene. She looked up in his face and asked a serious question.

"Are you going to be my daddy?"

Gene placed her on his knee and asked.

"Would you like for me to be your daddy?"

Nodding her little head yes, Gene made a priceless promise.

"Then Daddy, I am."

They hugged each other and she joyfully skipped back to her room. I fought back the tears as I held his hands and whispered, "thanks."

Marriage was discussed. Twice we almost went for it. Fear stopped me. Not just the fear of losing my military benefits. With the cost of medical care escalating, I couldn't afford to lose that. But what I really feared was this much ecstasy. This relationship was miraculously designed just for us. I was afraid that one day I would wake up and find that this was all an antic. Our courtship had it's level of uniqueness. Such as the nights when he couldn't fall asleep, he'd call me. I'd pray and sing him to sleep. I wrote a lullaby just for him.

"Yes Jesus Loves You"

> Ye--s Je-sus loves you, Ye--s , Yes He loves you,
> Ye-s Je-sus loves you, read your Bi-ble it will tel-ll you so.
> I--know He loves you, I-I know God loves you, I-
> Know He loves you, read your Bible it will tel--ll you so.

I would continue to sing until I heard him snoring. Often times he slept with the phone off the receiver. Gene affectionately nicknamed me "Saint Dee."

While doing my missionary work, keeping up with Devonne's school activities and a full time job, I managed to add a couple of counseling, Bible and social work classes to my schedule. This broadened my scope in the church as well. I was later ordained as an Evangelist. My initial sermon came from my favorite Book; The Book of Revelation. My topic was "No Benefits for A Counterfeit Life." Surprisingly Gene fitted himself into my endeavors. He helped with getting the elderly to and from their doctor's appointments or grocery stores, even joined in the prayers for the sick.

I'll forever remember the day when Gene felt the "spirit." I was doing a service out of town and he had accompanied me. The Lord used me mightily, as I was finishing my sermon I noticed

Gene was looking a little peculiar. I thought that I had embarrassed him, but as I approached him, he was sweating profusely through his suit. With tears rolling, he look at me and asked, "Dee, what is this? My feet want to move." All I could do was shout, "Get him Holy Ghost." Spiritually we became a team.

CHAPTER EIGHT

Devonne has finally reached adolescence. A great deal of her shyness has disappeared. She is now her own little person. Has excelled in her academics. She represented her school on two of the televised academic programs. Her thirteenth birthday was celebrated with a dinner party. Two of her preferred teachers were invited. One, her basketball coach did the honors of pinning the corsages. He was not her music teacher's choice colleague but they were both refined this day. Gene's mother's presence, truly brightened her day. She saw herself as one lucky young lady with three grandmothers to wish her many happy years to come. I secretly invited her little chum. They mutually shared a crush though neither would admit it. His calls were the first one in the morning and the last one at night, with at least one each hour in between. He and his family became acquaintances of ours. They owned a beach house in Annapolis, Maryland and invited us on some of their weekend trips.

An apple who didn't fall too far from the tree, Devonne knew her tolerances and didn't mind getting her message across by any means necessary. Our first and only school encounter started with me receiving a phone call from the principle of her Catholic High School. There had been a shoving match in one of her classes and her name came up in the middle of the melee. When I arrived she was standing in the principle's office, huffed and refused to sit. As the Sister was telling me the story, Devonne kept cutting in, "that's a lie," or "she's lying." Every mother knows her child. After listening to Devonne say that she was only trying to stop a small situation that was none of her business in the first place from escalating made sense to me. That was Devonne's persona. Her Bible teachings had taught her to "follow peace with all mankind." This meant to avoid confrontations. Maybe I hadn't emphasized strongly enough that you can't always stop others. Anyhow, I couldn't allow her to disrespect the Sisters. I tried to help by stating that "there must be a misunderstanding." Devonne wouldn't stand for that.

"There's no misunderstanding, she's just telling a lie," was her cogent reply.

My threats to punish her did not influence her to yield one bit.

"Mother! You told me that all untruths are lies. A lie is a lie, no matter who is telling it. If you want to punish me for telling the truth, go right ahead."

Looking into her trusting, teary eyes, I knew that all the facts were not on the table. Sure enough, a day or so later and additional investigation proved Devonne's accuracy. The Sisters attempted to make an apology, they were not accepted. Devonne felt that the facts should have been collected before she was accused of anything and the meeting was called.

Baffled by Devonne's strong willed attitude I called Sally for advice. I had to get the difference between a misunderstanding and a lie through to Devonne, also the fact that one in authority must be respected without her thinking that they are exempt from lying.

Sally's forthright suggestion was not helpful. "Leave that child alone; you can't beat yourself out of your child. That was a dose of your own medicine."

Yes, I was good for standing up for what I felt was right, no matter what the consequences were, but I didn't always tell the truth. Devonne would tell the truth oftentimes knowing that some form of punishment was inevitable. A prime example was the trip to New York that she and a few of her friends had gotten together to see a play. They were coupled with their adored ones and couldn't find a parent to chaperon. They got one of the girl's sister who was only two years older and was taking her boyfriend. Of course she wasn't allowed to go, but I had to chuckle within. If that opportunity had come my way at her age, I would have had a lie so straight the Pope would have Blessed me and sent me to New York.

Devonne's maturity came at the most needed time. She was capable of getting herself off to school, prepare light meals as well as light housework.

My obligations were suddenly halted when I became ill and under went two major surgeries. The first one was done at Malcom Grow Medical Center at Andrews Air Force Base and the second one was at Walter Reed Army Medical Center. I was out of work and church for approximately eight weeks each time.

Home or Devonne went lacking for nothing during my illness. Gene stepped in and cared for her as a good father would. Their daily hospital visits could be singled out by the laughter and foot patters coming down the hallway. Upon my discharges he nurtured me as well. He would call during the day to make sure that I was alright and resting.

After my convalescent period Our lives took on a faster pace. The three of us became passing ships. Devonne was preparing for her SAT's and looking at colleges. I was working at a HMO, attending her extra curriculum activities when possible and church events. Gene had taken on more contracts for his trucking business. Our time together was special but limited. We made sure if both could not attend Devonne's games, one would. My mother in-law became deathly ill during this time and called for us to come to the hospital. I had extended myself so until I had little sleeping time. I would grab a nap on my lunch hour or in a chair before going to work.

  We all gathered over Sally's on Devonne's prom night. Everyone had a hand in getting her ready for her big night. Beth applied her make-up, Sally did the last minute touches to her gown. Uncle Paul was giving advice on drinking only non alcoholic beverages. I was too excited to be of any real help. I paced the floor until her date arrived. Gene was just being the proud "papa." I snapped pictures as Devonne made her way down the stairs. Greeting her date, they were equally nervous as he placed her corsage on her wrist and she pinned his boutonniere. I held back the tears as I checked to make sure they had their tickets and money for prom pictures. We all kissed her good-bye and wished them a blissful night.

  Arriving home from the Baccalaureate Services we received the sad news. My mother in-law had passed. This devastated Devonne. On the day of the funeral Beth and Sally had to physically carry her from the funeral parlor. Her graduation meant nothing. She refused to march because her grandmother couldn't be there.

The summer months were filled with gloom. My conversations had to be carefully chosen. Gene had a way of getting Devonne to talk because they had something in common. Gene played basketball during his high school and college days. Having a love for the game he'd coached Devonne. They spent most of their evenings on the court. She was the shortest one on the court but she was the best point guard that her school had to offer.

I decided to do something inspiring for her. I gave her a three-in-one party; birthday, graduation and leaving for college. Family members, teachers and friends made this party a success. Gene's mother's presence sparked some glee. This was the turning point for Devonne. At last happiness could be seen over her once despairing face.

As time drew near for her to leave, she wanted to do something special for Gene.
She and I took Gene out to dinner, there she presented to him a scroll. She had written a tribute titled. "My Missing Rose."

My Missing Rose

"There will always be a tomorrow but yesterday can never

be recaptured. I've heard this throughout my childhood. Nevertheless, I had become somewhat despondent and wondered how life, as beautiful as it is, could be so cruel. My greatest desire was to have a father and mother to love me as my peers had. As you know my dad was killed, forcing mother to become a single parent. We shared many happy days, still I could sense mother's emptiness as she could discern mine. I had no one to call me "Daddy's Little Girl."

As time arose for me to start school I was optimistic, thinking this would fill both of our voids. The first year was fulfilling. I had new friends, mother got involved in the P.T.A. and other activities.

Our summers were always fascinating, especially when grandmother came over and mother would take us down South, to the beach or just a picnic in the park. Grandmother constantly reminded me of how much I resembled my father, right to my laughter and wittiness.

My second school year was disappointing. A black cloud swept over my life as we attended a school function which included both parents. I was the only child there without a father. Some of the children began to tease me. I was even called a "bastard." I wasn't sure of the meaning but it didn't sound to be complimentary. I felt that the world had abandoned me.

Mother tried to brighten my seventh birthday by arranging a celebration at the church. She had a dozen of roses delivered. I managed to fake the smiles to show my appreciation to her and the congregation. Something was missing. I saw the roses. I counted them. Yes, there were twelve but something was still missing. The fellowship hall was beautifully decorated, refreshments were plenteous, still, the congregation sang "Happy Birthday" to one miserable little girl.

At last, a heavenly angel waved her magic wand. The miracles began to flow. You and mother met and fell in love. Everyone said that you are the reincarnation of my dad, which was frightening in the beginning, then you became my dad. Suddenly school became attractive. I ran track, joined the drama club, sang in the choir, played basketball and soccer, wrote for the school paper, served on the student council and was acknowledged in the United States Achievement Academy Year Book. I've received many certificates and trophies. I owe this all to God, you and my mother. You two attended most of my games and all of my performances. If we lost or I fouled out of a game you were there to comfort me. If we won or the performance was a success you were there to praise me. I shall never forget the play "West Side Story", I had dual parts, the school gained recognition in the local newspaper and cable television. After my performance you and mom came to me with a dozen of roses. Yes, I counted them. There were twelve. Everything seemed so right.

You always had a special way of chastising. Whereas Mother did more yelling and direct punishing, you'd calmly say "let's talk about this and see why this happened." Rarely did you see fit to punish me. The one word you never failed to underscore was "THINK". You often said "if you think through a situation before acting upon it, more than likely you'll make the right decision."

Now my college days have arrived and I'm about to leave,

but not without a mother and a father. I didn't get the chance to know my biological father. No, I can't recapture yesterday, but somehow I believe that my dad is well pleased with you, my "miracle dad".

My tomorrows will always be appreciated. The spirit of my father will forever be in my heart, for it was his prayers and wishes that brought us this far, but for now I'd like to "Thank You" for being "My Missing Rose."

Gene, a heart of Jell-O, melted as he read his tribute. He knew that Devonne was humble enough to listen, but he had no idea that she had combed his counsel into her life. He spoke of the time when he first met her. How tiny and innocent she was; now she has grown up and ready for college. "It's like watching the bud of a flower flourish or the wings of a baby bird strengthen," was Gene's comparison. "Better still, and more deeply felt, is knowing that I had a part in her flourishing and strengthening."

I saw myself in my child. Like me she had carried so much pain inside. I also felt a slight bit of jealously, but my feelings no longer mattered. I was overjoyed just to know that my little once distraught baby had found what she was desperately seeking. I haven't been a perfect mother, I'd made some mistakes I know, yet, she found space to praise me.

CHAPTER NINE

Uncertainty on the home front was on the rise. My faith was being tested endlessly. My health wasn't the best. My relationship with Gene seemed to be drifting apart. He tried to assure me that this was only a figment of my imagination. It seemed as though he was placed in our lives for a season and that season was over. Neither of us shared that "have to see you" attitude anymore. While trying to work through this I was hit with a "double whammy."

Early one morning I was awakened by the ringing telephone. When I answered, there was a strange voice on the other end. A lady identified herself as a doctor from the University of North Carolina Hospital, in Chapel Hill, North Carolina. After verifying my identity, her voice became sympathetic.
"Your father is here in critical condition and he is asking for his daughters."

Knowing my health situation, I did not hesitate to promise the doctor that I would fly out on the next available flight.

I immediately called Beth. She wasn't available to leave with me because of her position on her job and a project that had a dead line. I flew out alone.

Sally and Uncle Paul had retired and now living in Burlington, North Carolina. She offered to go check on Daddy so I could stay home and take care of my health problems. My gut instinct said "go now." "The entire flight is only fifty-eight minutes, I can handle that," was my means of reckoning with Sally.

I was now living in Southwest Washington, over looking the Potomac River. I could see the airport from my front room. As I flew out that day my thoughts were intense. How would I greet "my daddy" and what will I say?

He to had given his life to Christ and was working diligently in his church. The year before I'd held a service in Fayetteville, North Carolina. He accompanied me there to hear me preach. After that high-spirited service we shared some time talking about the goodness of the Lord. He seemed to enjoy my company as well as my accomplishments but he was a little concerned about his pastor finding out that I was an Evangelist. His Baptist pastor didn't believe in women preachers. Though he felt that I was doing a great work he wanted to keep it a secret in our hometown.

I always wanted to have a heart to heart talk with Daddy but felt that the time was never right. I'd always hoped that he would start the conversation. Now he is calling for us on his death bed.

Sally picked me up from the Raleigh-Durham airport and drove me to the hospital. Arriving at the hospital, not knowing what to expect I had a silent prayer as I entered the front entrance. Sally noticed how much discomfort I was showing, she found a wheelchair and wheeled me to Daddy's room. With my Bible on my lap, I rolled close to Daddy's bedside. Three doctors were there talking with him.

Just to look at Daddy, except the noticeable weight loss, he didn't look sick at all. He was alert and oriented, didn't appear to be in pain. Sparks gleamed in his eyes as he greeted me. He had to fight for every breath as he introduced me.

"Look--a--here, my--bab-y girl. I knew--that you--would-get here. Docs,--this is my--baby, Dee--Dee, tell her--every--thing that-- you'll have --told me."

I shook each doctor's hand. His primary doctor, the lady spoke.

"Hello, I'm doctor (Her Name), I'm the one that spoke with you this morning. You have a very sick father here. Your dad have cancer of the esophagus and lungs. I'm sorry to say that it was detected too late for us to be of any medical help. We're keeping him as comfortable as possible with pain medication and oxygen. He is aware of his prognosis, his days are limited."

A lump rose in my throat. I didn't know how to respond to the news. Daddy was only eighteen years older than Beth and twenty years older than me. I knew that he was critical but I wasn't expecting death. I stood from the wheelchair, leaned over to kiss him. I saw water welling in his eyes. I heard the words coming from my mouth, but I don't remember saying them.
"It's ok Daddy, everything will be alright, I'm here now."

"Am I saying that he will be well again, or it's ok to die?" I asked myself. I spent every possible moment with him the following weeks. The hospital staff was exceptionally generous. I was put up in the nurse's dorm for a minimal fee. It was there in the hospital on the bottom floor. I was usually in Daddy's room by eight in the morning and spent anywhere from twelve to sixteen hours with him, leaving only for a meal or to take my medications.

We started our mornings with devotions. I would read Scriptures and we prayed together. He kept insisting that he was fine and felt no pain. He didn't want me to worry about him. Morphine was his pain medication and it was being administered through his IV. Because he felt no pain, he thought that he was better than what the doctors had told us.

Daddy was anxious to have our "over due" conversation. I'd been informed by his doctors that his oxygen was at its highest level, so I didn't want to exhaust him. However, one morning after our prayer he continued to hold my hand.

"I was hoping--that Little--Bit could be--here-for this--but I don't -- have much--time.

Watching him gasp for every breath I tried to stop him.

"Beth will be here in a couple of days." I assured him.

"No, I may--not be--here," he insisted.

"I should--have said--this--years ago, I don't--want to die-with this in--my heart. I failed---your mama--and the -both of you."

Again I begged. "Daddy don't do this to yourself. All of that is behind us now."

"Listen, --to me," he pleaded. I love--yo'll--I was--young--and scared. I didn't--know--a thing--about how to--raise yo'll. I wanted--so much--for you, I didn't --want to see--yo'll working--in a factory--or on a--farm, or cleaning --white folks-- houses for a-- living, --that's why --I didn't-- try to- stop you-- from moving --to Washington."

Hearing all of this opened so many wounds as well as my mind to the many times when I wanted to converse with him. I found myself apologizing for all the times that I had beaten him while he was intoxicated and the time that I tried to burn him up.

"Daddy I have wanted to say these words for years also. I'd always wished that things were different for us."

Squeezing my hands, he accepted all of the blame.

"No baby--you did--just what--you should have. I de-served--every--lick that you--put on me."

He even managed to crack a joke. "Boy, you--show 'nough---was a strong--little girl,--I'd put you-- up against --any man."

"Now we can thank God that all is well," I said as I kissed him on his forehead.

Two of his doctors walked in on the finale of our confessions. Observing a well over due bond being restored, one of the doctors said, "sir, you are a real trooper."

Daddy had been mindful of my pain. I had run out of pain medication but I didn't want that to be his worry. With tears streaming, he questioned his doctor. "Doc, you-say that --you can't do--anything--for me, --can you--please do --something for --my little girl?"

His doctor agreed to see me in the emergency room after finishing his rounds. I fought for strength as I left the room.

Deciding what to do or where to go, I made my way to the chapel. Now, nearly fifty years old, sitting on a pew in a hospital chapel, with the words "my little girl" still ringing loudly in my ears. They had come from "my daddy's" mouth and I welcomed them whole heartily. While sitting there I had a mystical outer body experience. I was taken back to my childhood. I heard a heavenly song being sung direct from the throne of God. The words I'd never heard before and haven't heard them since. They were soft and entrancing. I saw the angels singing to God, though I never saw God's face, just so much homage being rendered around this huge throne with the image of a man sitting high above everyone with his back toward to me. The brightness was almost impossible to look upon. I saw myself as a child moving among the cherubs, searching for someone. Amid my searching three angels surrounded me. They were not recognizable, not by face or gender but even in my numinous state I heard myself address them as Mama, Ma Martha and I. E. All of this seemed so authentic. I thought that I had died and gone to heaven. I was led back to my natural body by another angel. This one I assumed was Lewis. He held me differently than the others.

The amount of time spent in the chapel was not noted but I realized that it was all a vision when the hand of a hospital chaplain rested on my shoulder. The front of my dress was soaked with tears. Handing me a Kleenex, the chaplain led me to the alter and whispered, "let's pray about it."

Beth came in, we shared my dorm room and took turns sitting with Daddy. She wasn't much comfort because she is the nervous type, can't deal with sickness or death. Daddy was the hero here. Knowing that death was upon him, he never gave up or complained. He accepted his illness as something positive taking one day at a time.

It was evident that Daddy knew of his condition before we were told. A cousin had called us months earlier and told us that he was sick. When we visited him he told us that he was alright just a little set-back. He never told us about his cancer. Before his last trip to the hospital he had taken care of all of his final arrangements. He gave us stern instructions.
"My suit--is hanging--on my--bedroom door,--you can--take it to-- the funeral-- home. Every--thing else is---taken--care of.
Yo"ll--can put-- a flower --on my--grave if--
you wish."

On December eighteenth, two months after his diagnosis, Beth and I was about to leave for a flight back to Washingron. I promised him that I would be back in a couple of days and spend the holidays with him. This was the first time that he showed any sign of fear as he prophesied. "Don't--yo'll leave--today,--this is-- gonna be--the day."
I should have listened to the prophecy. Instead I convinced him that he would be fine until we returned.

Barely getting home from the airport, the call came to Beth's house. Daddy had passed.

"This is gonna be the day," hit me in the face when Beth called with the news.

In a cold, lonely, hospital room, miles from his hometown, neighbors and friends, I, the great missionary, known for helping everyone, had allowed "my daddy" to die alone. Not a final "good-bye."

Beth and Larue drove down. I was not able to take the five hour car ride. I went to Walter Reed, seeking more pain medication. There I learned that I had to have more surgery. I explained to the doctor that I had to get back to North Carolina right away for my father's funeral. In no uncertain language the doctor quickly replied. "I'm not being intentionally insensitive. But, If you don't get this taken care of, you will join your father."

"If you will just give me some pain medication, God and I will take care of the rest." I sharply responded. My request wasn't anymore intentionally disrespectful than his remarks. As he was writing a prescription he cynically murmured. "You're going to need God for that tumor."

I felt that I had betrayed Daddy by not staying with him until death. I was determined to make his funeral if I lost my life trying.

Forcing myself to repack, I felt that I had lost my "new best friend." We had made a strategically move in nurturing our friendship. Now this has all been wiped away, but not before the reconciliation of the hearts. I acknowledge this as a Blessing for us because many apologies have been buried in guilty souls, never to be forgiven.

Getting out of town became a dangerous mission. I decided to hail a taxi instead of calling one. I ran outside with a carry on, a suit bag, a hat box and a large shoulder bag. Just as I stepped on the sidewalk I was mugged in front of my complex. I knew that crime had risen for I had been robbed before, but never at eleven o'clock in the morning. A man grabbed me from behind and fought furiously for my purse and carry on. My screams summoned help from every direction. Our complex security person was almost within arms reach. A motorist made an attempt to run down the mugger but the theif out maneuvered everyone. Another helper called the police from his cellular phone. With all of my identification, credit cards and plane ticket now gone, I sat in the street and cried. I missed my scheduled flight and had to seek help from Services for Military Families and the American Red Cross. Due to the up coming holidays there were no flights to be had. I really felt bad when a couple had to be bumped for me to fly out.

Beth and Larue met me at the airport and we drove directly to the florist. They had made their selections, which were well suited. A heart shaped pillow of roses went inside the casket from his grandchildren. Beth had chosen a large heart with roses and carnations which matched the spray on the casket. My decision was not hard to make. As I stepped through the doors my eyes fell on a family circle arrangement. All red roses with a missing link of white roses and a white dove flying over it. I chose this one. The dove I'll always keep.

Daddy's funeral were everything that I had prayed for. The admiration of a regular church service. I was overjoyed to hear all the praises from Daddy's church family and friends. Many came to us after the service, expressing their sympathy and acknowledging Daddy's good deeds and kind words. Both young and old lives had been touched.

Daddy's life wasn't long but according to his church members and neighbors it was a powerful one in his last years. I only hope that he had found some private happiness.

I have a strong belief that we should live each day as if it is our last. James said it well in James 4:14.

> "Whereas ye know not what shall be on the morrow.
> For what is your life? It is even a vapour, that appeared for a little time, and then vanisheth away."

Good-bye Daddy.

From your little girl.

CHAPTER TEN

"Well Lord, here I am again. Hurting, both spiritually and naturally, all alone and wallowing in my misery." I whispered after hanging up the receiver from scheduling a date to be admitted in Walter Reed Medical Center for my third surgery. I'm a loner. I'm not one who must have a "best girl friend," to tell everything. I treat everyone the same, not getting close to anyone. I've found that the only one to tell everything to is Jesus. Because of my eccentricity I'm often misunderstood. I'd been singled out as being "stand-offish", or egotistical which is not me at all. I've openly made myself available for anyone who may need me day or night. I've also made it known that I do not appreciate chatty calls at any hour.

My early mornings were spent walking along the Potomac River around the wharf. I found inner sereneness watching the rippling water and the airplanes taking off or coming in across the river. An array of boats were docked along the quay. They bobbled enthrallingly on the water. The house boats were especially captivating. The very thought of living on the water is spirit strengthening to me. I was constantly dreaming of affording such comfort. Most of my praying, meditations and writing were done by the riverside.

As I was packing for my hospital stay Uncle Paul called with some disturbing news. Rev. Earl had committed suicide. "They say it was an accident, nevertheless, he's dead," was Uncle Paul's report. I was deeply sadden, even more upset about the rumors that were going around. Some said that he'd become depressed and just couldn't take life anymore. Others were saying that a family member had left some pesticides out in a juice bottle and he drank it by mistake.

I am not the one to judge but I do pray that however he died, he had an opportunity to ask for forgiveness of his unholy behavior. In his early years he'd demonstrated so many good qualities. Parishioners idolized him. I'd like think that it was an accident. It's hard for me to believe that all those faith stimulating sermons that Rev. Earl had preached could be reduced to suicide. Anyhow, Uncle Paul had called to see if I wanted to attend the funeral. He was going and offered me a ride. I declined his offer but sent my condolences. I didn't want to postpone my surgery again.

The right decision, I was later told. There was a sea of mourners, well into the hundreds. Uncle Paul never got inside the church. Dignitaries from all denominations had come to pay their respect.

On the eve of my admission I had become a little wearied. Maybe my spirit was still troubled about Rev. Earl's death. I felt a death spirit over me. I called a family conference and dinner. I made it clear that in case of my death I didn't want a funeral or any such gathering. I wished everyone to remember me as they knew me. This position I hold today. If the Veterans Administration take too long in assigning me a plot, buy one in a regular cemetery and bury me as quickly as possible. Formal death notices can be sent out next week, next month or next year, it doesn't matter. Following my "Home Going" orders we prayed and I served a royal dinner. "My Last Supper."

I was aware that Walter Reed was a busy hospital and I didn't expect the world to stop for me, but I had not expected to go through a game of perchance. I was prepped a total of three times, taken to the hallway of the operating room, only to be taken back to my room after waiting for hours. All of the excuses seemed legitimate and unavoidable but my strength was weakening.

I was highly embarrassed when I filed a complaint. A lady three beds behind me who happened to be white was taken in for her surgery. I attributed that to her skin color and all the decorations on her husband's uniform. When I was told that she was having orthopedic surgery which required an orthopedic surgeon left me very remorseful. I was grateful to get back to my private room. There I was able to repent of my bellicose disposition without disquieting the privacy of a roommate.

I had requested no visitors. The word "NO" was not upheld. Anyone with missionary/ministerial privileges could get in. My room became a sanctuary. Pretending to be asleep was my only means of privacy until visiting hours were over.

After days of suffering through pain, both mentally and physically I decided to confront God seriously. I knew that He knew my circumstances and the pain that I felt. Somehow I felt that writing it would be a mean of direct contact. I wrote a letter to God. First I repented of my sins, known and unknown, then I thanked Him for his many Blessings. I acknowledged my unworthiness and disobedience, both to Him and the doctors, yet, I wanted to remain within His will. If my suffering was meant to be, then give me strength to go through. If not, please take me to my heavenly home. I placed the letter under my pillow.

A profound sleep came without me having to ask for pain

medication. I can't recall ever having such a restful night. There were no dreams or any such disturbance.

The doctors were confounded when they were summoned to my room about daybreak and found that my tumor had pressed its way through my abdomen. I was immediately prepped for surgery so the doctors could clean the fissure and stop the bleeding.

I thought that I had joined Lewis, he was holding me in the spirit as I was awakened in the recovery room by a nurse. "Oh no, I'm still on planet earth," I reluctantly told myself.

Less than a week I was home, on the road to recovery with instructions rest and return for suture removal.

Before I could fully recuperate I was receiving upsetting calls from North Carolina. Aunt Mabel started laying her guilt tactics on me. "I took car' of yo'll when you couldn't do fo'yo' self, now I need yo'll he'e," was her way of asking us to move down.

Uncle Robert had passed a year or so earlier. He wasn't sick too long before he died. Pneumonia was listed as the cause of his death but I'm sure that it was secondary to his heavy drinking, smoking, and old age.

Beth was not in a position to up root her family. She had a prestigious job in the Federal Government, well on her way to retirement in a few years. Her family was still home and Larue was still driving long distant.

I was more or less alone. Devonne had finished school, had a job and her own place. My job as a health technician was not that important, I also had income that would be sufficient if I didn't work, so it was more sensible for me to make the move.

Aunt Mabel kept calling, at least weekly. I promised her that we would come down soon to see about her . She wasn't totally alone, her eldest sister was living next door in our old house. Her sister was the eldest but she had the full use of all of her faculties and they sort of looked after each other.

When Beth and I went to North Carolina to check on Aunt Mabel we found that she was somewhat physically and mentally incapacitated. She was suffering from dementia, but with her strong dogmatic attitude she felt that nothing was wrong with her.

We found out that her other siblings had been checking on her and a nephew of Uncle Robert was there at least every other day. Although, she'd told us that she had nobody to help her. After talking with her, I promised her that I would move down and help her. I asked her to give me about six weeks to settle things in Maryland.

Returning home and settling all of my affairs wasn't too stressful. I cleared my move with my pastor and church mothers as I asked them for their continued prayers.

I had a final check-up at Walter Reed and was given a clean

bill of health. I had my records moved to Ft. Bragg, even though the drive would be at least a two to two an a half hour drive from our hometown, that was the closest military hospital.

Sorting through all of my belongings was the greatest job. I gave Devonne a few pieces of furniture, also some to the Goodwill. I eliminated as much as possible so everything would be able to go in an eighteen foot U-Haul truck. I packed a little each day until everything was packed.

In all of my eliminating and packing, I could not bring myself to throw out the mail that I'd received from Lewis. I have every letter and card that he has ever written me. It is fragile now and yellowed but it has given me comfort when I was down and needed a good cry. Around our anniversary time, our birthdays, or his death date are the hardest time for me. That's when I'll pull out my plastic storage box and read a letter or two, then pray for more strength to continue. Lewis's death has been a wound that time has not been able to heal. Yet, through Christ I have been able to accept it, knowing that God does not make mistakes.

With all of the preliminaries out of the way, I sat a moving date. I decided to get a couple of the elders from the church to load the truck for me. I'd drive the truck down myself. Beth decided to take a weeks vacation and follow me in the car.

On the morning of my move I woke around three o'clock.

There was nothing else to be done. I started pacing the floor. My emotions were being tormented with doubts of making this move. I will be leaving my immediate family behind. When I first broke the news to Devonne she wasn't happy about it but accepted it because she knew that I was going to help someone. Beth had no real opinion because she and her family visited her in-laws rather frequently, we could get together at that time.

As I sat on my bedside chair convincing myself to go through with this move, my secretarial phone rang. The desk clerk announced.

"You have a visitor, should I send him up?"

I didn't have to ask who it was, I knew that it was Gene. I had no intentions of seeing him again, definitely not this day. I'd hope to move on quietly, leaving all emotions and mental baggage behind. Yet, I paused a second , then said, "yes send him up."

I had been telling Gene for the past six weeks that I was moving to North Carolina, he didn't take me seriously. When he stepped inside and saw all the packed boxes his eyes watered. Standing in my foyer we held each other and wept for at least an hour. No words were exchanged during our tearful evoking of memories. When we unlocked our arms and souls he held my hands and made one final affirmation and request.

"Saint Dee, I truly love you, promise me that you will take care of yourself."

Still sobbing, I promised. "I will, and promise me that you'll do the same. Always remember that God loves you." He walked out like a ghost. I fell against the closed door and prayed for strength.

Gene had been an exceptional spiritual companion. Our relationship is not comprehensible to the natural intellect. It wasn't a sexual thing. It's as though God had taken ex-lovers and resurrected us as brother and sister in Christ. Whatever had happened I realized that the memories will always be a part of me and I thank God for it.

Dawn was slowly breaking, I had a few hours before the elders were due. I decided to take my final walk along the river. It was quiet and peaceful. A few people were out moving about on the main street in front of my building. Early joggers were running along the path and one or two residents were out walking their dogs. As I walked toward my favorite spot, I stopped and leaned against the railing. The mild troubled water seemed to speak to me. I fixed my eyes across the river toward the sky. There I saw angels rejoicing. I started Praising God for His beauty, for I have truly seen Him in His Glory. My whole life rolled before me as though it was a movie, the good and the bad. I saw myself being born; an old midwife delivered me. How happy were my parents. Mama had problems with her pregnancies as well; that lead to her early death. From my birth there was an extra hand holding me. During all of my grief, pains, depression, and disappointments I was never really alone. The Lord's hand followed me; He fought all of my battles. As rebellious as I had been, God never gave up on me. I thanked Him for having faith in me when I didn't care to listen to Him.

> My eyes have seen the glo-ry of the com-ing of the Lord, He is tram-pling out the vin-tage where the grapes of wrath are stored: He hath loosed the fate-ful lightn-ing of His ter-rible swift sword-His truth is march-ing on
> Glo-ry! glo-ry, hal-le-lu-jah! Glo-ry! glo-ry, hal-le-lu-jah! Glo-ry! glo-ry, hal-le-lu-jah! His truth is marching on.
>
> In the beau-ty of the lil-ies Christ was born a-cross the sea, With a glo-ry in His bos-om that trans-fig-ures you and me; As He died to make men ho-ly, let us die to make men free, While God is march-ing on.
> Glo-ry! glo-ry, hal-le-lu-jah! Glo-ry! glo-ry, hal-le-lu-jah! Glo-ry! glo-ry, hal-le-lu-jah! His truth is marching on.
> Julia Ward Howe

I must have been elevated in the spirit. The clapping of five onlookers quickly drew me to my earthly state. According to their accounts I'd loudly sang the "Battle Hymn of the Republic" in its entirety. Hearing this, all I could say was, "To God Be The Glory."

Author Biography

E. Nadine Thaxton-Tensley, now resides in Maryland, a Viet Nam widow, mother of one daughter, an evangelist, working in the Church of God In Christ Inc., a student with hopes of becoming either a Certified Health Care Administrator or Physician's Assistant.

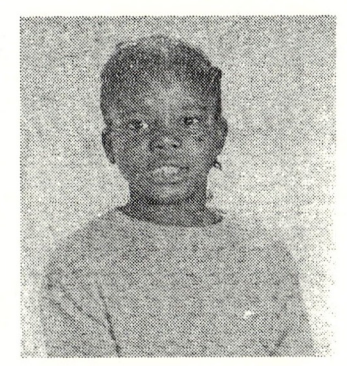

Nadine was educated through the District of Columbia Public School System. She continued her education through the GI Bill. Her studies took her into a few areas, but because of her upbringing and belief in Christian values she chose to work in health care where she is quietly able to administer God's Love.

Printed in the United States
42083LVS00004B/271

9 780977 229680